Songs of Praise
A Christmas Companion

For Carodyce, Charles and Jeremy, who
introduced me to Christmas.

Text acknowledgments

pp. 62, 110: Extracts from the Authorized Version of the Bible (The King James Bible), the rights in which are vested in the Crown, are reproduced by permission of the Crown's Patentee, Cambridge University Press.

pp. 12, 44: Extracts from *The Book of Common Prayer*, the rights in which are vested in the Crown, are reproduced by permission of the Crown's Patentee, Cambridge University Press.

pp. 21, 47, 50, 56–57, 60, 78: Extracts from the Revised English Bible with the Apocrypha copyright © 1989 by Oxford University Press and Cambridge University Press.

p. 31: 'Like a candle flame' by Graham Kendrick. Copyright © 1988 Make Way Music, PO Box 263, Croydon, Surrey CR9 5AP, UK. International copyright secured. All rights reserved. Used by permission.

p. 38: 'Advent Calendar' by Rowan Williams, from *After Silent Centuries*, published by Perpetua Press, 1994. Reproduced by permission.

p. 48: 'The Coming' by R.S. Thomas, from *The Later Poems of R.S. Thomas, 1972–82*, published by J.M. Dent.

p. 56: Extract from 'Who put the colours in the rainbow?', words by Joseph Arthur Paul Booth, copyright © Paul Booth. Administered by CopyCare, PO Box 77, Hailsham BN27 3EF, UK, music@copycare.com. Used by permission.

p. 63: 'Christingle Carol', words by Basil Bridge (1927–), copyright © 1990 Oxford University Press, from *New Songs of Praise 5*.

pp. 69–70: 'Shepherd's Pipe Carol', words by John Rutter, copyright © 1967 Oxford University Press. Reproduced by permission.

pp. 88–89: 'The Sheepdog', copyright © U.A. Fanthorpe, from *Christmas Poems*, 2002. Reproduced by permission of Peterloo Poets.

p. 123: Extract from 'God Knows', a poem by Minnie Louise Haskins, 1908. Published privately in *The Desert*.

pp. 124, 125: Extracts from 'The Flight into Egypt' from *For the Time Being* by W.H. Auden, published in *Collected Poems*. Published by Faber and Faber Ltd and used by permission.

p. 128: 'No Small Wonder', words copyright © Paul Wigmore/Jubilate Hymns. Used by permission. (The choral setting for this Christmas carol, published by Animus, is by Paul Edwards.)

Picture acknowledgments

Picture research courtesy of Zooid Pictures Limited and Lion Publishing.

AKG – Images: pp. 34–35 (Erich Lessing).

Andrew Barr: pp. 3, 4, 7, 14–15, 20, 23, 27, 41, 42, 64, 72–73, 75, 76, 80, 81, 86–87, 89, 92–93, 94, 106, 112, 115, 126.

Bridgeman Art Library: p. 52 (Palazzo Medici-Riccardi, Florence, Italy).

Corbis UK Ltd: pp. 8–9 (Martin Jones), 11 (Archivo Iconografico, S.A.), 46 (R.W. Jones), 58–59 (Alissa Crandall), 61 (Philadelphia Museum of Art), 109 (Christie's Images).

Lion Publishing: pp. 1 (David Townsend), 16, 31, 38, 105.

Peak Pictures: pp. 48–49.

Rex Features: pp. 82–83 (Jonathon Player), 98 (Nils Jorgensen), 123 (Stephen Meddle).

Scottish Viewpoint: pp. 118–19 (Andrew Wu).

Succession Picasso/DACS 2003/Artothek: p. 68 (copyright © Succession Picasso/DACS 2003/Artothek).

Songs of Praise

A CHRISTMAS COMPANION

ANDREW BARR

A LION BOOK

A Lion Book
an imprint of
Lion Hudson plc
Mayfield House, 256 Banbury Road,
Oxford OX2 7DH, England
www.lionhudson.com
ISBN 0 7459 5126 0

First edition 2003
10 9 8 7 6 5 4 3 2 1

By arrangement with the BBC

BBC logo © BBC 1996
Songs of Praise logo © BBC 2000

The BBC logo and *Songs of Praise* logo are trademarks of the
British Broadcasting Corporation and are used under licence

A catalogue record for this book is available
from the British Library

Typeset in 11/14 Berkeley Oldstyle
Printed and bound in Singapore

Contents

• • • • • • • • • • • • • •

Preface

· · · · · · · · · · · · · ·

Each Christmas Eve, the sound of a familiar radio broadcast brings back a childhood memory of my mother. She is precariously balanced on a wobbly chair, willing sprigs of holly to stay in place behind the mirror in our front hall, while through the atmospherics of our valve radio, as if from very far away, a small, pure voice begins to sing, 'Once in royal David's city stood a lowly cattle shed...' That afternoon, the nine lessons and carols from King's College Chapel, the college's annual gift to the people of Cambridge, had become BBC radio's gift to us at home, and it was my introduction to broadcasting the Christmas story.

I think I was born with a map and a timetable clutched in my hands. Since my childhood, I have been addicted to travel. Growing up in flat London suburbs, my best memory of church as a child was when we sang the Advent hymn, 'Hills of the north, rejoice'. Now that I live in those northern hills, I must visit the 'isles of the southern seas'. Now, as then, I am intoxicated by the thought of a journey.

When I can no longer travel, I hope that I shall at least be within tottering distance of some great cathedral. Recently, I drove home from Kent to Scotland up the Great North Road, which takes you past some of the most beautiful cathedrals in the land, like great ecclesiastical service stations, and I made my own service break in York Minister for choral evensong. On a chilly Sunday in January, we strangers, many of us passing through on our way to somewhere else, entered in dribs and drabs and scattered ourselves around in the peculiarly Anglican way. At 4 p.m., when we stood for the entrance of the choir, I realised that there were actually two or three hundred of us gathered in this casual way. 'Full house,' my neighbour observed. As the quarter chimes of the Minster clock ended, and the deep boom of Great Peter, the biggest bell in England, sounded out the hour to the city, a voice near us sang in the purest tones, 'O Lord, open thou our lips…'

The daily 'moving travellator', as one bishop described cathedral worship, is familiar to anyone who works in broadcasting, another constantly moving process. For more than 80 years, BBC religious programmes have helped audiences travel through the seasons of the year, and especially during the short days and long, dark nights of winter, when many turn to television and radio for company.

This Christmas companion to *Songs of Praise*, a series that has itself been on the move for more than 40 years, not only around Britain, but around the world, is the story of two journeys. The first is a journey of several thousand miles in autumn and winter, beginning when, as J.B. Priestley put it, '… the red ruins of autumn were still about us'. I travelled away from the Midlothian hills of home to the mountains of Bosnia and Slovenia, by  way of the most westerly tip of Cornwall, then flew home and meandered back through the home counties of England, the Midlands, East Anglia, the North-East and finally the capital city of Scotland.

The second voyage is one we can experience together, a journey through time, to take us through the weeks of Advent leading up to Christmas and on to Epiphany, to arrive with the wise men at the stable in Bethlehem. Sometimes, it is a journey through times remembered, of Christmas past, not least for me of 30 years of producing *Songs of Praise*.

Behind the big event of each programme, from some beautiful church or
cathedral, are the smaller episodes and experiences of the community that
lives and worships there, which every producer hopes will add up to a
deeper meaning. And that is how I hope my collection of stories and
journeys in *Songs of Praise: A Christmas Companion* will strike the reader.

Many have offered me kindness and hospitality on the way, and particular thanks are due to Hugh Faupel and Michael Wakelin of BBC Religion, who now share the task of running *Songs of Praise*. A big thank you also to Pamela Hossick, one of the new generation of television directors, and her team, who let me eavesdrop in Salisbury Cathedral.

I am grateful to the Reverend Keith Watson of St Hilary's, Churchtown, in Cornwall, and to Donald Reeves, former rector of St James's, Piccadilly, who have introduced me to people in both Britain and Europe whose stories will make ideal contributions to future episodes of *Songs of Praise*. Morag Reeve, Jenni Dutton and Nick Rous at Lion Publishing have again been wise and imaginative editors and designers.

In the fast-changing world of broadcasting, *Songs of Praise* alters, but I hope it will never lose a certain quality, which, long ago, the writer H.V. Morton found in the traditional English village:

That village, so often near a Roman road, is sometimes clearly a Saxon hamlet with its great house, its church and its cottages. There is no question of its death: it is, in fact, a lesson in survival, and a streak of ancient wisdom warns us that it is our duty to keep our eye on the old thatch, because we may go back there some day, if not for the sake of our bodies, perhaps for the sake of our souls.
FROM *IN SEARCH OF ENGLAND* (1927) BY H.V. MORTON (1892–1979)

In the musical celebrations of *Songs of Praise* at Christmas, as an old story is retold, new ones are beginning. I hope that this book, like each programme, may help you find your own part in both.

ANDREW BARR
January 2003

ADVENT

The Annunciation by Fra Angelico (c. 1387–1455).

Waiting

● ● ● ● ● ● ● ● ● ● ● ● ●

chapter one

STIR UP, we beseech thee, O Lord, the
wills of thy faithful people; that they,
plenteously bringing forth the fruit of
good works, may of thee be plenteously
rewarded; through Jesus Christ our
Lord. Amen

COLLECT FOR THE TWENTY-FIFTH SUNDAY AFTER
TRINITY, FROM *THE BOOK OF COMMON PRAYER* (1662)

How many family cooks today still think of the collect for the
twenty-fifth Sunday after Trinity as a kindly reminder by the vicar
to 'stir up' the ingredients for the Christmas pudding? Rather than
that old chestnut from the pulpit, it is more likely to be the effect of television
and radio cascading information at us from all directions that will stir us up
these days. In our present hyperactive age, we need to be stilled more than to
be stirred up. How can we make room for the great religious feast of Christmas
and its prelude, the waiting time of Advent, to plenteously reward our lives?
How can we quieten the excitement bordering on panic that is stirred up by
the media, with their promises of unending entertainment and relentless
'shopping days to Christmas' countdowns?

Television and radio programmes are not the most obvious places to
look for stillness, although even there, there are voices speaking about the
yearning for it. During the weeks before Christmas, listeners to the *Daily
Service* on Radio 4 will be encouraged to look for stillness in prayers and

music, and in the Bible stories of the prophets and people who foretold what would happen in the stable at Bethlehem. And even the most secular news bulletins will sometimes include reports intended to offset our headlong rush into the season of goodwill.

Pictures and sound have the potential to create almost any mood, and even to reveal hidden depths of meaning, but ways to convey stillness and silence are elusive. It is far easier, particularly with such a fast-paced medium as television, to portray excitement and noise. As a television director of religious programmes, I have tried again and again to find ways to produce moments of stillness on the screen. With talented cameramen, I have searched for images that will offer viewers a space for meditation on their own story as the Christmas story begins. I have never really succeeded.

The late Canon Frank Wright tried to do it in the 1980s with his *Meditation* on ITV. There would be minutes of silence as the camera showed the cross on the high altar of Manchester Cathedral, and in the foreground a kneeling figure. For a decade, *This is the Day*, the BBC's Sunday worship programme from a viewer's home, always included the meditation image of bread and a Bible, with a flickering candle in the room repeated into infinity on the television screen. Even *Songs of Praise* sometimes includes brief glimpses of calm. Framing and focusing on those beautiful, familiar shots of carol singers in ancient cathedrals, the producers know that time spent in preparation of heart and soul may keep us all from ending up totally exhausted by Christmas Day. But none of us has discovered how to convey the stillness of one line from 'O little town of Bethlehem': 'How silently, how silently, the wondrous gift is given!'

In life, moments of stillness arrive unexpectedly. Near our home, there is an old wood that sometimes provides such moments. Even our ancient collie-cross stray, committed to a lifelong campaign of frantic, nose-to-the-ground scavenging, will sometimes for no apparent reason raise his failing eyes and stand motionless for a few seconds. Here, I am surrounded by autumn stillness, such a deep stillness that on a windless day, when a last golden-brown leaf drops from a branch, I almost hear it sigh as it twists and flutters to the ground.

A last, beautiful leaf, with its delicate veins, has fallen, unprompted by rain or even the faintest breeze. It is a mystery to me why this moment is its last. I find myself jogging back to childhood and to almost the same experience on another late-autumn day, walking on a Kentish common with my father.

Mine was a suburban childhood. Mostly, our Sunday-afternoon walks in the gathering gloom were dull and uneventful. My late father was a man of few words when it came to thoughts and feelings. Without a dog to walk, we still had to be 'done good', so we plodded silently around lamplit suburban roads and through parks where all the leaves had been methodically tidied away. As a schoolboy, I used the flyleaf of a Bible to cross out days and months of such routine dullness. Just occasionally, we would explore further afield. Several miles away was the common.

This was *Just William* territory, for his creator, Richmal Crompton, lived nearby, and it was where she wrote her wartime stories of William and the Outlaws in search of spies. Among the young birch trees, my father and I reached a quiet, still place where once had been the anti-aircraft gun emplacements where my father had served during the Blitz of 1940.

On this particular Sunday in November, weeks after Remembrance Sunday, my father paused and broke his customary, rather gloomy silence to remember with grim humour the time when his platoon had come to this same spot on the common to set up camp in a big bus marked 'Troop Movements –

Secret'. And a moment later, as we stood silently together, contemplating the follies of war, a leaf fell. And broke the silence.

Someone in broadcasting once told me that the microphone had been perfected to capture just such a minute sound, but it hasn't, and nor has any television camera so far caught the experience of such a moment. My father and I had reached what David Stancliffe, the current bishop of Salisbury, who has led the team creating the Church of England's new services, calls the

'hinge-point' in the year. On that dark November Sunday, All Saints' and All Souls' Days being long past, the church's Advent, the Christian new year, was just beginning. For us, it was signalled by that shared moment of stillness as the last leaf fell. We both felt it. As we waited on the common under a gas light for the hourly Sunday bus to take us home, we moved from crossing out days of mundane routine to ticking off days of excited anticipation of Christmas.

Today, in the woods with my old dog, and old enough myself now for pessimism and panic to be closer to what I usually feel at the coming of Christmas, the quiet fall of the last leaf has once again restored in me a sense of tranquillity and wonder.

The suburbs are the place where most of us still live. Fifty years ago, the architect J.M. Richards was in the Holy Land, the strangest of locations from which to write *The Castles on the Ground*, a meditation on English suburban life. 'In suburbia,' he wrote, 'nothing is not subject to the Englishman's determination and control... the suburb is a world peculiar to itself and – as with a theatre's drop scene – before and behind it, there is nothing.' The writer evoked a world that I knew well:

The street is hushed, so that the footsteps of a late visitor ring sharp and distinct, and so does the sing-song voice calling a dog in repeated summonses from the shadows of a barely visible porch. Nor can anything be seen to move, except when the headlamps of a car passing the end of the road throw a beam of ghostly light in quick succession over tree and hedge and porch and lamp post, to die away on the edge of the pavement.

He described a wandering pilgrim walking the Sunday-evening streets, pausing to view home life through the as-yet-uncurtained front windows. This was a better-than-television experience, and one that my father and I often shared. The drama witnessed through these windows often came back to me later, when directing *Songs of Praise*. And it had been a salutary glimpse for a would-be television director of how little attention most people at home actually paid to what was on the screen, even when gathered with the lights off around the flickering, fuzzy, black-and-white images of the 1950s' sets.

Many years after those suburban walks with my father, during an autumn when I was struggling to learn the seemingly impossible skills needed to direct television cameras and living a charged-up life that denied any moments of stillness, I returned one afternoon to the common. I found again the quiet birch wood where the guns had been placed to defend London. This time, it was not a leaf from a tree but the leaves of a Bible that provided the 'hinge-point'. Preparing to direct a live Sunday-evening television programme about the Bible, I had bought myself a copy of the recently published New English Bible. Reading the Old Testament in modern English was like a door opening into a new world. Instead of listening to someone else reading elegant but old-fashioned poetry from a lectern in church, I was for the first time reading the ancient prophecies in a language I could easily and completely understand. Unexpectedly and unintentionally, back in the suburbs I had grown up in, I experienced again a sense of the beginning of Advent.

Every year on dark winter nights in this season, through the words of the carols sung on *Songs of Praise* or *Sunday Half-Hour*, or by the little group of carol singers huddled on the pavement outside our doors, there is strange news for the suburbs of a birth in the Holy Land. According to the story that we are about to hear once again, it will change the world.

I looked from afar
And lo! I see the power of God coming
And the cloud covering the whole earth.

Go ye out to meet him, and say,
'Tell us, art Thou He that should come
To reign over Thy people Israel?'
High and low, rich and poor,
One with another.
Go ye out to meet him, and say,
'Hear, O Thou, Shepherd of Israel,
Thou that leadest Joseph like a sheep,
Tell us, art Thou He that should come?'

Stir up Thy strength, O Lord,
And come to reign over Thy people Israel.

FROM THE ADVENT RESPONSORY

The Journey Begins

WHEN HANDEL, in his sublime moods,
dissolved his hearers into ecstasies, he was
said to bring all heaven before their eyes.

SAMUEL LANGFORD (1863–1927) IN THE *MANCHESTER GUARDIAN* (1927)

Surely Samuel Langford, one of the *Manchester Guardian*'s greatest
music critics, was thinking of the *Messiah* when he wrote these
words in his last review before his death. I always imagine that
he had an English north-country landscape in mind when talking about
heaven, as he had heard Handel's great oratorio performed in proud
northern towns like Huddersfield, with its famous choral society, so
many times. Corporation halls would become the Jerusalem of the
Pennines whenever the tenor soloist rose to sing, 'Comfort ye, comfort
ye, my people.' Then the air would continue with Isaiah's great prophecy,
'Every valley shall be exalted.' Each winter in Langford's day, every
northern valley would be exalted by the airs and arias and above all by the
great choruses of the *Messiah: Part One* as the biblical story leading up to
the birth in the stable was told.

Music is the perfect travelling companion, especially on a long
winter's car journey, and I relive those moments from the *Messiah*
whenever I drive through the countryside of the north of England. Britain's
motorways are rarely portrayed as places of romance on television, but as
a film director, I have always wished I could have made the documentary
about the building of the trans-Pennine M62 in the 1960s, which was

shown on ITV at the time. As people and machines invaded the fells, the civil engineer spoke of his 'vision' for a new highway to link the lands of the white rose and the red rose forever. Meanwhile, the sound of Handel came bursting through the roar of machinery, suitably interpreted by a bluff northern soloist, accompanied by a brass band. Today, the mountains and hills have been 'made low and the crooked straight', and the drive through that dramatic landscape is effortless. Perhaps, one day, the producers of *Songs of Praise*, who are based at the BBC in Manchester, will be inspired by the unfolding landscape, which they see as they hammer along motorways to witness the nation singing, to plan another great Advent *Messiah*. For it is somewhere in these hills, thanks to Handel's sublime composition and his unmistakable interpretation of England's north country, that heaven is brought before our eyes.

The trans-Pennine M62.

A voice cries:
'Clear a road through the wilderness for the Lord,
prepare a highway across the desert for our God.
Let every valley be raised,
every mountain and hill be brought low,
uneven ground be made smooth,
and steep places become level.
Then will the glory of the Lord be revealed
and all mankind together will see it.
The Lord himself has spoken.'

ISAIAH 40:3–5

It is a rainy lunchtime on the M6, when the weary travellers draw into the motorway service area to be met by sounds of Christmas. 'O come, all ye faithful' is playing just loudly enough to trigger a desire for seasonal shopping. And it is only November. Yet even though this is the wrong time to be listening to this carol, it may be the right place, high on Shap Fell on the edge of the Lake District, to think about a strange legend associated with those familiar Christmas words.

In Advent 1745, Bonnie Prince Charlie passed this way with his rapidly disintegrating army. This was a change of fortune for the Jacobites. Since 31 October 1745, the prince and his followers had seemed unstoppable as they headed south from Edinburgh towards London and King George II. They had reached Derby on 4 December 1745, but in the absence of additional support from the English Jacobites and a French invasion, they had decided to retreat. The story goes that 'O come, all ye faithful' was the coded rallying call to the Catholic prince's cause. It is not completely implausible. The carol first appeared in 1743 as *'Adeste Fideles'*. The translation came from the pen of John Wade (c. 1711–86), a Catholic who lived and worked in both France and Lancashire. At that time, the planned surprise invasion of England from France was only cancelled due to storms in the Channel. Looking across the damp and inhospitable fells today, I wonder where Wade was during Advent 1745, when the Jacobite army was horribly bogged down as they struggled north to Penrith and Carlisle. Eventually, they were defeated at the Battle of Culloden on 16 April 1746. Their cause was lost, but the carol they sang survives, and for us today it has the universal meaning that makes Christmas Christmas.

Back on the M6 this November, as articulated lorries hurtle south, laden with dozens and dozens of neatly cut Christmas trees, far from looking forward to Christmas, we are still waiting for Advent, the season that offers Christians the time and space to prepare themselves for the great festival. How long will our resolution to make space for Advent last this year?

Immediately, there appears another premonition of Christmas, as a cloud of pure white smoke drifts slowly up Shap Summit: a steam train of a sort rarely seen here since the 1960s is climbing through the landscape towards us. For the younger generation, it could only be the Hogwart's Express, taking Harry Potter and his friends home from wizard school for the Christmas holidays. But those of us who remember *Children's Hour* on the radio 50 years ago may think of another steam-train journey in John Masefield's *The Box of Delights*. The adventure begins when young Kay Harker is joined by two sinister clergy on his train journey home for Christmas, from Musborough Junction to the cathedral city of Tatchester. I can still remember the sleeplessness of the winter nights that followed each cliffhanging episode, and I never hear the sound of the harp picking out the tune of 'The First Noel', in Victor Hely-Hutchinson's *Carol Symphony*, without thinking of that most evocative serial.

The brilliant sound effects were as menacing as in any modern mystery movie, as Kay, helped by the old magician Cole Hawlings and his Barney dog, takes on the forces of darkness. Kay's first encounter is with Chubby and Foxy, his sinister clerical travelling companions, who, under the malign influence of Abner Brown, a wizard craftily disguised as the Reverend Dr Boddledale of the Missionary College, planned to ransom the Christmas celebrations in Tatchester Cathedral in exchange for the 'Box of Delights'. Unless this evil gang were given the magical box, which contained the elixir

of eternal life, the
bishop, dean, chapter and the entire choir
would be consigned to a watery grave, and Christmas would be
cancelled forever. Here is Abner Brown at his most evil:

Abner Brown: *I shall have more – I must have more! 'Infinite riches in a little room,' as the poet says. And I shall have them – or under Condicote Weir goes that shining brood of Merry-Christmas shepherds! I shall flood them to eternity!*

'Where Alph, the sacred river, swishes,
with Organist and Boys and Bishes,
down to a sunless sea!'…

Narrator (Kay Harker): *It was all clear – all devilishly clear! The return of the entire cathedral staff, or their death by drowning under the mighty sluices… and all in exchange for Cole's elixir and the Box, wherever it might be – and that was, of course –*

Kay Harker: *With me! It's only… with me!*

Narrator: *And I remember, to this day, the small, lost sense of an immense responsibility that was suddenly in me. There was only one course: to go, myself, to that great underground network of caverns under the Missionary College by the weir itself. To go swift – and to go small… And as I did, I remember praying:*

Kay Harker: *'O Greatness, hear, O Brightness, hark,*
leave us not Little, nor yet Dark!'

FROM THE RADIO ADAPTATION BY JOHN KEIR CROSS (1911–67)
OF *THE BOX OF DELIGHTS* (1935) BY JOHN MASEFIELD (1878–1967)

The story of *The Box of Delights* was – and still is – in a funny way, just right for a child's-eye view of Advent, but especially so in the austere post-war days of food rationing and power cuts, when it really did seem as if Christmas would never come.

O come, O come, Emmanuel,
and ransom captive Israel,
that mourns in lonely exile here
until the Son of God appear:
  Rejoice! Rejoice! Emmanuel
  shall come to thee, O Israel.

LATIN (18TH CENTURY), TRANSLATED
BY J.M. NEALE (1818–66) AND OTHERS

Oxen and Candlelight in the Garden of Devon

• • • • • • • • • • • •

chapter three

CHRISTMAS IS COMING,
the goose is getting fat,
please put a penny in the old man's hat;
if you haven't got a penny, a ha'penny will do;
if you haven't got a ha'penny, God bless you!

BEGGARS' RHYME

A dvent Sunday dawns in the South Hams, bringing with it one of nature's rare winter blessings, for yesterday's dark, damp, mist-soaked hills have been transformed under cover of darkness. Dried by a blustery wind from the south-west, the beauty of the wild Atlantic coastline that leads into Salcombe's natural harbour is unveiled as the sun slowly rises into a clear, ice-blue sky. Even without the Advent story, daybreak like this would seem to signal a fresh beginning. On this Sunday, the flag of St George streaming in the wind from the top of the tower of Salcombe's parish church and the bell-ringers hard at work in the belfry all announce across the rooftops that the church's new year has begun.

Down below, in the still, shadowy canyon of Fore Street, the Christmas-lights committee is also hard at work. For them, there is no time to lose as they lay out their long strings of brightly coloured lights, which will illuminate the little street in celebration of Christmas. A giant, light-filled cracker lies on the pavement, ready to be hoisted into position; and above the post office flies a ruddy-faced Santa, whose friendly but fixed grin could never match the cheerful faces of the volunteer team of fishermen and tradespeople swinging him into position. A plaque on a wall near the jetty records an award to the many volunteers of Salcombe for their community spirit. The Christmas lights will help dispel the Scrooge in all of us, and the money we drop into their collection buckets over the next weeks will make possible many unexpected acts of kindliness to the housebound and the homeless.

It is no easy task to put up strings of Christmas lights in an increasingly blustery wind. The volunteer who has gingerly climbed to the top of the ladder has to be reassured by a stream of banter from a colleague on the bottom rung, for he is very high and the street is very narrow and still open to traffic. All is well until a friendly wave to a passing motorist tests their goodwill: the distracted driver accidentally steers straight over the string of lights still lying in the road. A pedestrian hurrying by on his way to church turns a deaf ear to the sudden chorus of down-to-earth expletives and silently commends the team, and thousands like them all over Britain, to the good Lord for their charity.

Up in the church, as the congregation arranges itself around the nave in the familiar, scattered disposition never seen on *Songs of Praise*, the sun catches a stained-glass nativity scene. There is to be a nativity play here next week, but there are a thousand and one other events also to come, as the priest taking the service ruefully remarks, plunging into a formidable list of announcements. Then comes a moment of quiet and stillness, and the choir sings:

This is the truth sent from above,
  the truth of God, the God of love;
therefore don't turn me from the door,
  but hearken all, both rich and poor.

The first thing that I will relate,
that God at first did man create;
the next thing which to you I tell –
woman was made with him to dwell.

Then after that 'twas God's own
choice
to place them both in paradise,
there to remain from evil free
except they ate of such a tree.

But they did eat, which was a sin,
and thus their ruin did begin –
ruined themselves, both you and me,
and all of our posterity.

Thus we were heirs to endless woes
till God the Lord did interpose;
and so a promise soon did run:
that he'd redeem us by his Son.

Holy Trinity, Salcombe's parish church.

And at this season of the year
our blest Redeemer did appear,
and here did live, and here did preach,
and many thousands he did teach.

Thus he in love to us behaved,
to show us how we must be saved;
and if you want to know the way,
be pleased to hear what he did say.

ENGLISH TRADITIONAL

'It is the Garden of Devonshire,' wrote Mr Marshall, an economist, of the South Hams in his *Rural Economy of the West of England*, published in 1805. However, he first visited the area on Christmas Eve 1799, arriving in an open carriage 'in the teeth of one of the severest winds that ever blew over the face of this county'. He was glad of the shelter of the high hedges of the South Devon lanes, but he noted that 'these unfriendly fences would be embarrassing to an invading army'. He was thinking of the threatened invasion by Napoleon's troops, not the army of tourists who now invade the countryside – but he was right.

When he returned in 1804, again in Advent, he noted that, astonishingly, swallows and house martins were still evident that December, and the thrush had been heard singing in every month of the year. But it was the sound of the human voice that inspired Mr Marshall to write with uncharacteristic lyricism. At that time in Devonshire, oxen were still used for ploughing, turning over the rich, red earth ready for future planting. Watching them at work, Mr Marshall wondered whether horses might not be more efficient, but he wrote:

The style of driving an ox team here is observable; indeed, cannot pass unnoticed by a stranger. The language, though in a great degree peculiar to the county, does not arrest the attention, but the tone or tune in which it is delivered.

The plowboy chants the counter tenor with unabated ardour, the plowman throwing in his hoarser notes. It is understood that this chanting march, which may sometimes be heard to a considerable distance, encourages and animates the team, as the music of a marching army, or the song of the rowers.

The sound reminded him of a cathedral choir, and so perhaps provides a clue as to how the singing for Advent and Christmas may have sounded in nearby Exeter Cathedral at the time. This Advent Sunday, on a walk after church, the fields are silent and empty, the ploughing having already been completed by now-inanimate farm machinery. The sounds of the 19th-century oxen team and singing ploughboys and ploughmen at work in the lea of oak, beech and larch trees, originally cultivated for the naval shipyards of Plymouth, are all gone forever.

So as my wife, Liz, and I walk home for tea, we must be content with the televised sound of cathedral choristers in *Songs of Praise* from Blackburn, Lancashire. Blackburn has an important part in the history of *Songs of Praise*, because when the programme went through its greatest transformation in 1977, to include filmed interviews of local people talking about their faith and choosing the hymns, this cathedral was the first to take part. The then-choirmaster, John Bertalot, drew an electrifying sound from a huge congregation, largely made up of church choirs from all over Lancashire. Shy people who had never spoken in public, and singers who had never dreamed of being heard by an audience larger than a church congregation, found themselves talking about their most profound beliefs and singing hymns to an audience of millions on television.

As *Songs of Praise* has shown time after time, both in the interviews and in the singing, we can all surprise and surpass ourselves. Advent tells us that even the hoarsest, housebound non-singer has their part to play in the coming of the kingdom of God, and it is definitely as a hoarse, though not housebound, non-singer that I play my own part later that night in the Advent carol service in Malborough, the next village down from Salcombe.

The night is dark as we make our way through a rising gale to All Saints' Church, which describes itself as 'the cathedral of the South Hams'. The light in the 13th-century porch is a welcome sight for visitors who have forgotten that on moonless nights the country walker had better carry a torch. Inside, some of the morning's bell-ringers from Salcombe have reassembled, although the wind must be whipping the sound of the bells straight off to Dartmoor. As we find a place towards the back of an already-full church, the choir is gathering behind us at the west end of the 15th-century nave, its low arches faintly illuminated by many candles. We in the congregation are also given our own candles, as yet unlit.

We stand in the dark as the choir sings the Palestrina setting of words from the Advent Responsory, 'I looked from afar'. Then comes Sally's moment. Sally will carry the processional cross as the choir moves up the nave to its normal place at the east end, but first, as the candlelit choir clusters round her in support, she begins her solo verse: 'O come, O come, Emmanuel…' When the choir comes in with, 'Rejoice! Rejoice! Emmanuel shall come to thee, O Israel,' and begin their slow procession up the central aisle, there is evident relief that she has sung so well. We are now so used to the icy perfection of broadcast singing performances that this is a moment to remember and treasure, of someone not famous, or on television, but singing beautifully and from the heart for the benefit of her home community. And so it will be for the hundreds of other brave young amateur soloists on whom we rely each year to begin 'Once in royal David's city' in the traditional way.

Now a frail brightness spreads through the nave as neighbours in the pews light each other's candles, and we are all able to join in the final verses of the Advent hymn.

How different evensong would have sounded in Mr Marshall's day, and how much the hope of Advent must have meant then to parishioners gathering on a dark night in Devonshire, wondering whether the threatened French invaders were already on their way. Sometimes life reminds us that Advent, a time of hope, can also be dark and dangerous. The battering wind irritates us tonight as we leave the church, but it would have reassured Mr Marshall's 1804 congregation to know that any enemy sailing towards them would surely have been dashed to pieces on the treacherous rocks of the South Devon coast.

While we have been singing in the candlelight, the Christmas-lights committee in Salcombe has finished its work and decided to go the whole hog. All the lights are up and ablaze, and the town is ready to party. Our grandsons have been busy while we were out, writing a long list of requests in anticipation of our Christmas gifts. Back at our hotel, the restaurant pianist is way ahead of us all, dreaming of a white Christmas.

The bright lights of Salcombe and our flickering candles in the ancient darkness of Malborough tell us that now, as in the past and as in the future, however dark and dangerous the world may be, God is with us.

Graham Kendrick's carol is like an Advent prayer for Christmas:

Like a candle flame,
flick'ring small in our darkness,
uncreated light
shines through infant eyes.

Stars and angels sing,
yet the earth sleeps in the
   shadows;
can this tiny spark
set a world on fire?

Yet his light shall shine
from our lives, Spirit blazing,
as we touch the flame
of his holy fire.

God is with us, alleluia,
God is with us, alleluia,
come to save us, alleluia,
come to save us, alleluia!
GRAHAM KENDRICK (b. 1950)

Light of Lights

• • • • • • • • • • • • • •

chapter four

ETERNAL RULER of the ceaseless round
of circling planets singing on their way;
guide of the nations from the night profound
into the glory of the perfect day;
rule in our hearts, that we may ever be
guided and strengthened and upheld by thee.

J.W. CHADWICK (1840–1904)

There had never been a painting like it, some said, when it was first shown to the world in 1764. On a huge canvas, almost seven feet wide and five feet high, now on view in Derby Art Gallery, a small group of people gathers around an 18th-century machine called an orrery. An orrery displayed the 18th-century astronomer's knowledge of the motions of the planets and the sun. Its elegant frame held brass balls representing all the then-known objects in space and was kept in motion by a concealed clockwork motor.

In the picture, there is a demonstration in progress. While the children seem enraptured and the adults engrossed by what they see, the lecture has been stopped for questions by the man on the left, whose note-taking seems to be distracting the lecturer. I have always assumed him to be a journalist.

A Philosopher Lecturing on the Orrery was painted by Joseph Wright of Derby (1734–97). I first looked at this picture in the 1960s with self-declared humanist Dr Jonathan Miller, one of the stars of *Beyond the Fringe*, who was presenting an arts programme. As the sound recordist on the shoot, I enjoyed his formidable gift of mimicry when, between takes, he would lampoon many well-known characters. Most frequently, he would assume the voice of the then-chairman of the BBC, Lord Hill, in his wartime role as the 'radio doctor'. But when he wasn't startling us with his enquiries about our bowels, Jonathan was also encouraging each of us in the crew to find our own way of looking at this painting.

It is not the 18th-century scientific view of a mechanical universe that I find so interesting, but the painter's extraordinary ability to depict light. The small group has gathered at night, and there is only one source of light, which the artist has prevented us from seeing: a dark, silhouetted figure in the foreground blocks our view. What we can see, however, is the dramatic effect of the light reflected off each figure, revealing the expressions on their faces as they look at something wonderful – something they have never seen before. It is my icon for Advent.

It is a painting for every film or television director trying to learn more about the potential of light. Twenty-five years ago, Ray Short, the first series producer of *Songs of Praise*, came up with the suggestion that I should make an Advent *Songs of Praise* on the theme of light. It was to be made in Clare College, Cambridge, where the 18th-century chapel has retained all the rationalist elegance of Joseph Wright's day. Appropriately, the dean of the college at the time was Dr Arthur Peacocke, who has since won the Templeton Prize for his lifetime's study of the relationship of science to religion.

The dean was firm in his insistence that *Songs of Praise* from Clare College should not be illustrated by any Christmas-card angels. He chose to welcome viewers to the programme by reading from the Elizabethan founder's charter that the college 'should assist true religion and further public good and give light to those who walk in the dark paths of ignorance'.

As I set out to make *Songs of Praise* by candlelight for the first time, it was the perfect opportunity to see if modern technology could depict light as Joseph Wright had done 200 years before.

Songs of Praise directors have always had to accept the limitations of technology, but they are more fortunate today than the television pioneers of the 1930s. When, on Christmas Day 1936, the choirboys from St Mary of the Angels Song School broadcast carols from the BBC at Alexandra Palace, the cameras were so insensitive to light that the boys had to sing, caked with make-up and dripping with sweat, under the ferocity of hundreds of lamps as hot and bright as the midsummer sun at noon. Up until 1977, the first generation of *Songs of Praise* directors had to carefully plan how to show the grandeur and beauty of historic churches without the cameras being blinded by the huge banks of lamps needed to light the congregation, for whom it was often a tropical experience.

During our Clare College recording in the winter of 1977, singers needed to have pullovers on under their cassocks for the very first time. In the chapel, there was nowhere to suspend scaffolding for lamps, or room for large television cameras. We used two small film cameras loaded with a new kind of colour film, which was far more sensitive to low light, and apart from a handful of small lamps, the cameraman, Keith Hopper, wanted to rely on candlelight.

It was to be a most unnerving experience. The technology that would allow us to make a continuous recording had not yet been developed, so each shot had to be filmed separately. Consequently, the programme was made in small pieces that could be stitched together later in an editing suite. Unlike with today's autofocusing home-video cameras, Keith had to focus and adjust every moment and every move by hand, as he squinted through the tiny eyepiece of his viewfinder.

A Philosopher Lecturing on the Orrery (1764–66) by Joseph Wright of Derby (1734–97).

Both participants and crew had to imagine themselves into an experience of Advent, which, only a few years later, director Chris Mann was almost magically able to achieve in one evening with a large outside-broadcast unit in Salisbury.

And unlike a normal *Songs of Praise*, which would be directed through headphones from a mobile control room outside the church, I had to direct this programme by crawling around the chapel floor and pointing silently at the shots I wanted. Moreover, this had to be done without distracting the performers or gaining the disapproval of the eagle-eyed and rather fierce Dr Peacocke.

That we did not destroy the atmosphere we were trying to create was almost entirely due to a promising young conductor called John Rutter, today the distinguished composer of many popular carols. John was angelic, exuding both calm and enthusiasm through many long hours of fragmentary recording. Fresh supplies of candles had to be produced constantly. Carols had to be sung again and again. Even when we reached the end, we had to wait several nerve-racking days while the film was processed before we were certain that anything had come out.

I reminded John of his seraphic demeanour when I visited him in his medieval home near Cambridge a quarter of a century later. Although he was counting down to conducting the world premiere of his *Mass of the Children* at Carnegie Hall in New York, John concentrated with a great intensity as, through an archive videotape, we were both transported back to 1977's Clare College Advent *Songs of Praise*.

'Look at their long hair,' laughed John, whose own hippy hairstyle on the day was never revealed on the screen. As the conductor, he had been determined to remain invisible so that the programme could communicate worship rather than performance. There in the candlelight were all the young, anxious faces of the student singers, John remembering each of them by name.

There was Kit Hesketh-Harvey, of *Kit and the Widow*, cabaret artist and

now master of avoiding 'hesitation, repetition or deviation' in Radio 4's
Just a Minute. There was Harvey Brough, later to become Harvey and the
Wallbangers; Paul Daniels has gone on to be principal conductor of the
English National Opera; Simon Buttress is well known on the West
End stage; and Ivor Bolton, who played the organ in spite of incipient
bronchitis, now conducts the Mozartean Orchester in Salzburg. So many
hopeful beginnings captured in our candlelit shots.

There was one moment that came close to the enchantment of Joseph
Wright's painting. A burning taper was passed around as each person in the
congregation lit their neighbour's candle. As the light spread, it illuminated
their faces one by one.

In the glow of the candlelight, we recognised those who had taken
part in the programme by talking about their faith in the midst of the
daily life of the college. One person brought light in both image and
word: Professor C.M. 'Charlie' Moule, theologian and former dean of Clare
College. In 1977, he had already been a fellow for 33 years, and today he
is still hale and hearty in his nineties. As he walked in Clare College garden
between smouldering piles of autumn leaves, he spoke about Advent:

*This lovely garden reminds me of something which I am deeply convinced of:
that if you believe in God at all, then you are bound to believe that he is in the
whole of his creation and shows himself in everything that one sees. Now I am
also reminded in this season that God isn't at all limited to beauty. Because if the
Christmas message means anything at all, it means that God comes as a helpless
human being and simply puts himself at risk and exposes himself to all the dangers
of being human, and to the poverty and to the darkness and to the danger.*

Looking again at the Joseph Wright painting, I wonder about the human
figure silhouetted in the foreground. Are they blocking the light, or did
they bring it with them to light up the clockwork orrery, that earthbound,
mechanical depiction of the heavens?

At the 2002 Advent carol service in Clare College, the choir sang words written by another former dean of Clare College, one who is now archbishop of Canterbury:

He will come like last leaf's fall.
One night when the November wind
has flayed the trees to bone, and earth
wakes choking on the mould,
the soft shroud's folding.

He will come like frost.
One morning when the shrinking earth
opens on mist, to find itself
arrested in the net
of alien, sword-set beauty.

He will come like dark.
One evening when the bursting red
December sun draws up the sheet
and penny-masks its eye to yield
the star-snowed fields of sky.

He will come, will come,
will come like crying in the night,
like blood, like breaking,
as the earth writhes to toss him free.
He will come like child.

'ADVENT CALENDAR' BY ROWAN WILLIAMS (B. 1950),
FROM *AFTER SILENT CENTURIES* (1994); SET TO MUSIC
BY CHRIS BROWN FOR THE 2002 ADVENT CAROL
SERVICE FROM CLARE COLLEGE, CAMBRIDGE

The Holly and the Elder

chapter five

LO! HE COMES with clouds descending,
   once for favoured sinners slain;
thousand thousand saints attending
   swell the triumph of his train:
     Alleluia!
   God appears on earth to reign.

Yea, amen, let all adore thee,
   high on thine eternal throne:
Saviour, take the power and glory,
   claim the kingdom for thine own;
     O come quickly,
   Alleluia! Come, Lord, come!

CHARLES WESLEY (1707–88)

Billy McCormack is steeped in the old ways of rural life in the Scottish Lowlands, where he was born and bred. As an elder of a country kirk, his duties include ringing in Christmas and the New Year, but he seems happiest hard at work in the open air. In the first year since he retired as a parks head gardener, nurturing greenhouse plants for display all over Midlothian, the list of people he is now helping out in their own gardens grows longer by the day.

Each December, Billy can be found surrounded by sacks of moss, holly branches with and without berries, laurel, yew and even discarded hedge trimmings, all gathered from the surrounding countryside, with which he will make 100 Christmas wreaths. His annual foraging is no threat to the environment, for his are not the mass-produced efforts of the commercial garden centre. Each one will be individual, some a mixture of plain and variegated evergreens, some finished off with a flash of red ribbon, the most beautiful adorned with white lilies. One of the best will be presented to the manse.

Once upon a time, every kirk elder would have had a copy of *The Manse Garden* on their bookshelf. This slim volume first appeared in the 1860s, and it was written by a Presbyterian minister who felt so guilty about allowing himself to be diverted from the care of souls by the care of plants that he wrote under the pseudonym of the Reverend N. Paterson, DD. 'The Author', he explains in his preface, 'expects, by hiding for a little, to give the arrow less nerve, because the bowman can only shoot into the air, not knowing whither to direct his aim.'

'Of all the trees that are in the wood, the holly bears the crown,' goes the Christmas carol, and the 'Reverend Dr N. Paterson' agrees. Anyone keen to trace the old manse garden of the anonymous minister will only need to search Scotland for a 19th-century garden surrounded by holly and liberally shaded by a large holly tree, which 'in winter provides shelter when all other species, in their cold nakedness, offer nothing'. As Paterson advises:

Plant hollies and every inconvenience will disappear. It is the laurel of Burns, and the sanctuary of singing birds. Shielding its songsters from the hawk, it shelters them in the storm, and feeds them with its fruit when other trees are bare. It does one's heart good to see the humble blackbird pecking a red berry amidst the falling snow.

This year, Billy McCormack has borrowed our far-from-capacious greenhouse to work in and filled it with his berried holly to prevent already well-fed garden residents from snacking on his works of art. The other ingredients are piled up in sacks outside. Every day but Sunday, he is hard at work from first light. 'This is the old way of doing it,' he says, telling me how he was taught to make his first Christmas wreaths almost 50 years ago by Harry Anderson, head gardener at Oxenford Castle. 'In Harry Anderson's day, it was a much harder job to be an artist. We used "jaggy" holly and thick twine, and you couldn't make many without your hands being cut to ribbons.' These days, he uses a holly called 'half-in-half', which appears to be a less prickly variety.

When Billy began to make wreaths for the village of Pathhead, he was

only making a dozen or so. But the demand soon increased, and he was asked for more and more each year. When he reached 100 wreaths, he thought it was time to think of the future, so he taught one or two of the young men in the village how to do it. Now many of the front doors in the village are hung with locally made wreaths at Christmas.

He works at a steady speed all through Advent, first 'mossing' each ring, woven from coppiced branches, then deftly winding on bunches of evergreen. 'The only thing that can hold me up is a hard frost attacking the ingredients.' Slowly, through the December days, his pile of completed wreaths mounts up beside the greenhouse, covered each night with a green tarpaulin.

Watching Billy at work seems to put us in touch with an older wisdom. When the wreaths are all collected, leaving our winter garden suddenly bare, we discover that many of them are going to the local graveyard. The families and friends of Christmas past are not forgotten, and many of Billy's regular customers lay their wreaths on the family grave faithfully each year. Billy's finest wreath will lie on his sister's grave.

The holly and the ivy,
when they are both full grown,
of all the trees that are in the wood,
the holly bears the crown:
O, the rising of the sun,
and the running of the deer,
the playing of the merry organ,
sweet singing in the choir.
TRADITIONAL FOLK SONG

Today, this carol that Cecil Sharp, a collector of folk songs, first heard in the Cotswolds 100 years ago is a familiar part of everyone's Christmas celebrations. But it is probably far more ancient in origin, the holly symbolising the masculine and the ivy the feminine elements, and the whole being sung to a pagan dance between the men and the women. It is easy to imagine the forebears of Billy McCormack taking part in the ancient ceremony. Billy and his wife Margaret rarely let a Saturday night pass without joining friends for traditional Scottish country dances. And the forebears of that anonymous minister in his manse garden would surely have encouraged both dancing and 'sweet singing in the choir'. As the Reverend Dr Paterson says, 'It is the holly, always inspiring as all other things decline, which alone can make the progress of shelter keep pace with the progress of time.'

chapter six

Dot.com

● ● ● ● ● ● ● ● ● ● ● ● ● ●

BLESSED LORD, who hast caused all holy
Scriptures to be written for our learning:
Grant that we may in such wise hear
them, read, mark, learn, and inwardly
digest them, that by patience and
comfort of thy holy Word, we may
embrace and ever hold fast the blessed
hope of everlasting life, which thou hast
given us in our Saviour Jesus Christ.
Amen.

COLLECT FOR THE SECOND SUNDAY IN ADVENT,
FROM *THE BOOK OF COMMON PRAYER* (1662)

One late-autumn Sunday, about 20 years ago, in an ancient country-parish church in Kent, something odd happened. Hymns had been sung and matins was almost over, with only the vicar's sermon and closing prayers to come. But the vicar, instead of going to the pulpit, went to the vestry and emerged with a toy gun, which he waved in the general direction of the choir. Two of them, he announced, in the bogus guttural tone more usually found in a Len Deighton spy movie, were being arrested for being in possession of illegal literature. 'Look at this,' he said, and with almost convincing indignation held up what looked like a Bible.

It *was* a Bible, and before we could stop him, the vicar had ripped it in half and thrown it up in the air. Thus, a rather sleepy country congregation was quickly woken up to the reality of life for many Christians who were still, even in those days towards the end of the Cold War, being persecuted for their faith. (But as they say on children's television, don't try this at home – brandishing even a toy gun in church today would be a serious criminal offence.)

The end result of our normally gentle vicar's startling foray into melodrama was a big response to his appeal for Bibles to be collected and sent to countries in Eastern Europe. It also marked the successful launch of a scheme dear to his heart: to put a Bible into every pew of our own church. A mere week or two later, on Bible Sunday, the second Sunday in Advent, the late Donald Coggan, who had just retired as archbishop of Canterbury, joined us for a dedication service for our new pew Bibles. He warned us never to see the Bible as merely part of our English way of life – something we all had but took for granted, like our parish church, our digestive systems or the *Radio Times*.

Christmas is the one time in the year when *Songs of Praise* celebrations include scripture readings. Usually, these are done by celebrity actors who prefer, in imitation of Alec McCowen, who famously learned the whole of Mark's Gospel by heart in order to perform it on stage, to learn rather than read their passages. This is often done against a background of guttering candles in the cathedral crypt, or while wandering soulfully about the cloisters – the Bible as performance art, not the familiar companion on the way that it is for so many Christians. But then, how many of us ever actually open our old family Bibles and sit down in a quiet corner to read again the wonderful Christmas story as the great day approaches? I can only remember one *Songs of Praise* interviewee, or indeed anyone, who can claim to have read the whole Bible in one sitting. He was a coach-tour driver who had found a copy when he went to the back of the coach for a nap while waiting for his passengers. He found himself reading it from beginning to end.

Probably most of us would look up our favourite passages, a habit first formed in the 17th century when those stalwarts of *Desert Island Discs*, the

Bible and Shakespeare, first became easily available to the general public. As a result, the first 'anthologies' appeared, those collections of 'the flowers of the verse' as the Puritans described them. These days too, *Songs of Praise* regularly takes the form of an anthology, weaving together prose, poetry and music.

Minister and hymn-writer John Bell, in an Advent programme, took up the literary metaphor, describing the old-age pensioners of Luke's Gospel, Elizabeth and Zechariah, Simeon and Anna, as 'the bookends of Advent and Epiphany'. He said these 'are people who are forgotten in the story of Christmas. But God puts a new value on people who think they are past it, people who have got stuck, and he expects those who are in their senior years to be the midwife of the new thing that he wants to do.' Being one of

those whom John Bell would describe as 'up in years', I appreciate Luke's inclusion of these old people.

Luke describes his purpose in the opening verses of his Gospel:

Many writers have undertaken to draw up an account of the events that have taken place among us, following the traditions handed down to us by the original eyewitnesses and servants of the gospel. So I in my turn, as one who has investigated the whole course of these events in detail, have decided to write an orderly narrative.
LUKE 1:1–3

And so the Gospel writer took on a task familiar to today's television producer, making sense of many fragments of stories that he has heard in order to reveal the big picture.

'On the Sunday in the year when traditionally we give thanks for the Bible and especially the Old Testament, I would like to say something about dots and an umbrella.' So Gilleasbuig MacMillan, minister of St Giles's Cathedral, Edinburgh, began his sermon on Bible Sunday. He had our attention. The umbrella was disposed of first, in a story about a man waiting in a bus queue in a rainstorm, his brolly neatly furled and protected against the elements in case it was needed in the future. It was a puzzle whose meaning we were meant to work out for ourselves.

And the dots? He said Bible stories are like the dots in a puzzle. Preachers choose all sorts of different ways of joining them up to make their own pictures and patterns. The Jewish rabbi will not make any sort of pattern from the Old Testament that points to Christmas. The 17th-century preacher would join his dots to make a portrait of the God of battles. In our own time, at last, the God of hope for the whole world's blessing is beginning to appear in the dots.

This is the age of 'dot.com' revolution, rapid communication by computer, instant access to almost anything, almost anywhere in the world. And news is another bewildering dot-joining process. The images on our television screens are formed from millions of whizzing electronic dots, which tell myriad human stories, and each viewer must join up these dots too, to make sense of the pictures. Sometimes, in this strange, new, non-linear digital-media world, it is as if the Bible is the only sequence of dots that does make any sense.

And God held in his hand
a small globe. Look, he said.
The son looked. Far off,
as through water, he saw
a scorched land of fierce
colour. The light burned
there; crusted buildings
cast their shadows: a bright
serpent, a river
uncoiled itself, radiant
with slime.

*   On a bare*
hill a bare tree saddened
the sky. Many people
held out their thin arms
to it, as though waiting
for a vanished April
to return to its crossed
boughs. The son watched
them. Let me go there, he said.

'THE COMING' BY R.S. THOMAS (1913–2000),
FROM *THE LATER POEMS OF R.S. THOMAS, 1972–82*

chapter seven

Angel Voices

· · · · · · · · · · · · · ·

IN THE SIXTH MONTH the angel Gabriel was sent by God to
Nazareth, a town in Galilee, with a message for a girl betrothed
to a man named Joseph, a descendant of David; the girl's name
was Mary.

The angel went in and said to her, 'Greetings, most favoured
one! The Lord is with you.' But she was deeply troubled by
what he said and wondered what this greeting could mean.
Then the angel said to her, 'Do not be afraid, Mary, for God has
been gracious to you; you will conceive and give birth to a son,
and you are to give him the name Jesus. He will be great, and
will be called Son of the Most High. The Lord God will give
him the throne of his ancestor David, and he will be king over
Israel forever; his reign shall never end.'

'How can this be?' said Mary. 'I am still a virgin.'

The angel answered, 'The Holy Spirit will come upon you,
and the power of the Most High will overshadow you; for that
reason the holy child to be born will be called Son of God.
Moreover your kinswoman Elizabeth has herself conceived a
son in her old age; and she who is reputed barren is now in
her sixth month, for God's promises can never fail.'

'I am the Lord's servant,' said Mary; 'may it be as you have
said.'

Then the angel left her.

LUKE 1:26–38

As a religious broadcaster, I have come across many strange stories of people who believe they have been visited by angels. What makes Mary's experience, as told by Luke, unique is that the angel Gabriel was not there for Mary alone, but to bring his message to every one of us. As theologian and broadcaster Dr Colin Morris puts it, 'With an utter uniqueness, God is about to break into our human history.'

But does the profound story of Mary's visitation by an angel mean that we should also believe that we each have 'guardian angels'?

Hollywood's answer to the angel question rejoiced in the name of Clarence Oddbody. 'I'm the answer to your prayer,' he told George Bailey, the hero of *It's a Wonderful Life* (1946). Frank Capra's classic movie nearly always gets a television airing around Christmas. Every year, we seem to switch on just in time for this thoroughly sentimental tale, and we can never leave the room until it finishes, to the accompaniment of some epic nose-blowing to conceal our tears.

The film tells the story of homespun, nice-guy George, a.k.a. James Stewart, who finds himself in desperate financial trouble. Everything he tries to do to put things right only makes things worse, and as the Christmas snow falls, a despairing George decides to throw himself into the river. Just as he is about to jump, another man falls in, and George instinctively dives in to the rescue. The stranger is Clarence, the second-class angel, who has yet to 'earn his wings'. Clarence tells him, 'I jumped in to save you, George: it's against the law to commit suicide where I come from.'

George tells him bitterly, 'I wish I'd never been born.' So Clarence shows George his home town as it would have been if he *had* never been born – a far unhappier place, because the good turns that George has done throughout his life have changed everything for the better. The film, of course, has the happiest of endings: George begs, 'Help me, Clarence! I want to live again!' And waking as though from a dream, he runs back to his real life and home, prepared to face the music – but he finds instead that everyone in the town has clubbed together to settle his debts.

'Choir of Angels' (c. 1460), fresco by Benozzo di Lese di Sandro Gozzoli (1420–97). Detail from the *Journey of the Magi* cycle in the chapel, Palazzo Medici-Riccardi, Florence.

There is a heavenly postscript for Clarence too. When a small bell on the Christmas tree begins to ring, George's little daughter tells him, 'Every time a bell rings, another angel gets his wings.'

'Attaboy, Clarence,' says George.

Well, was it only a dream? A few years ago, this was the question we put to people living in Scotland, who told us their own stories of meeting angels on a religious programme I made for ITV, part of a series called *Moment of Truth*. In Glasgow's Barlinnie prison, a young man serving a life sentence believed he had seen an angel, as did a professional woman in Falkirk, when she was ill at home, and a young boy who had been agonisingly burned in an accident in the kitchen.

Keeping an open mind, we asked the advice of a psychiatrist, who was also a church minister. He told us:

One in six of the population will see or hear something from 'elsewhere', and these are perfectly normal people. These angels may be tall and surrounded by light, but above all, most of the figures are clothed in our own ideas and thoughts and in what we have been taught. What we expect is what we see.

The prisoner alone in his cell was less interested in the burnished wings of his visitor than in the conversations they shared. 'It was an angel that made me aware that there is good in me, and the important thing in the world for me is to save my own soul.'

In Falkirk, the camera showed the street where our next witness said that, at a time of great despair, she had seen a mysterious, tall figure dressed like a man at arms, wearing an exquisitely beautiful breastplate, standing outside her window. 'I'm not given to wishful thinking, and not very often do 10-foot neighbours in the Roman army come and stand outside my gate. But I knew somehow that he represented God and that he was there on my account.'

The terrible pain that young Colin felt when he burned his hands suddenly faded as he saw what he calls 'an image' in the room. 'It was clothed and human-sized but without wings. I can't really describe it, but it was light and lovely and suddenly I wasn't scared.'

His mother, who had been desperately cuddling him, praying in panic, had opened her eyes to find Colin grinning. 'Mum, the pain's gone. It's all right.'

One thing all these mysterious stories had in common was that the angels were present at a moment of crisis. They were guardian angels like Clarence, sent to save one particular person. Even a cynical and sceptical television film crew had to admit that life for all our storytellers, just as for George Bailey, was utterly different by the time their 'angel' had left them.

St Augustine wrote:

Angel is the name of their office, not of their nature. If you seek the name of their nature, it is spirit; if you seek the name of their office, it is angel; from what they are, spirit, from what they do, angel.

Somebody once analysed the lyrics of pop songs and discovered that the word 'angel' was contained in one in ten songs. So it is not surprising that on one of Scotland's main pop-music stations, the volunteers who help out in a weekly phone-in programme are also affectionately known as 'the angels'.

These 'angels' are the people who answer the telephone for Andrew Monaghan's 'Open Line', a live phone-in broadcast every Saturday night between 11 p.m. and 2 a.m. on Radio Forth. For over 20 years, people throughout the east of Scotland have been telephoning Andy, telling him, and each other, about their troubles, hopes and fears. These are people whose voices are rarely, if ever, heard anywhere else in the media – frightened, muddled and lonely people. Some are regulars, often sufferers from depression or from various forms of addiction; others will be calling for the first time, as a last resort when all hope seems lost. The volunteer 'angels' behind the scenes, who will have listened to the story before Andy takes the call on air, will often have been the first people to make a difference. Sometimes, with the presenter's non-judgmental encouragement, callers come back the following week, or months or even years later, to say they are getting better, that they can see light at the end of the tunnel.

One Saturday night in Advent, Joan calls in to say she has come through 10 years of depression, feels better and looks forward to Christmas. Bob wants us to think about the children in countries where there are wars, who won't be having a happy Christmas. And, unexpectedly but appropriately for the season, Matthew is on line four to say that he is happy that his girlfriend is pregnant, but he wants to know how to make things right with his upset mother. Later, the girlfriend is on too. She says that she is pretty scared, and concerned about her dad. Says Matthew, 'We live in an awful small house, and I'm worried about getting this straight before she's due.'

I believe an angel helped them all.

chapter eight

An Interview with God and Mr Noah

• • • • • • • • • • • • •

WHO PUT THE COLOURS in the rainbow?
Who put the salt into the sea?
Who put the cold into the snowflake?
Who made you and me?

J.A.P. BOOTH

All through a long autumn night in Slovenia, near the border with Austria, a terrifying storm has become trapped by the mountains that surround the miniature paradise of Lake Bled. Nobody in Tito's old summer palace, now a luxury hotel on the shores of the lake, can possibly be asleep. For what seems like hours, I lie rigid on my bed while the thunder crashes and lightning flashes flare across the room, triggering apocalyptic thoughts about Noah and the flood:

God said to Noah, 'I am going to bring the whole human race to an end, for because of them the earth is full of violence. I am about to destroy them, and the earth along with them. Make yourself an ark with ribs of cypress; cover it with reeds and coat it inside and out with pitch. This is to be its design: the length of the ark is to be three hundred cubits, its breadth fifty cubits, and its height thirty cubits. You are to make a roof for the ark, giving it a fall of one cubit when complete; put a door in the side of the ark, and build three decks, lower, middle,

*and upper. I am about to bring the waters of the flood over the earth to destroy
from under heaven every human being that has the spirit of life; everything on
earth shall perish…*

*In the year when Noah was six hundred years old, on the seventeenth day
of the second month, that very day all the springs of the great deep burst out, the
windows of the heavens were opened, and rain fell on the earth for forty days and
forty nights…*

*The flood continued on the earth for forty days, and the swelling waters lifted
up the ark so that it rose high above the ground. The ark floated on the surface of
the swollen waters as they increased over the earth. They increased more and more
until they covered all the high mountains everywhere under heaven. The water
increased until the mountains were covered to a depth of fifteen cubits. Every
living thing that moved on earth perished: birds, cattle, wild animals, all creatures
that swarm on the ground, and all human beings. Everything on dry land died,
everything that had the breath of life in its nostrils. God wiped out every living
creature that existed on earth, man and beast, creeping thing and bird; they were
all wiped out over the whole earth, and only Noah and those who were with him
in the ark survived.*

GENESIS 6:13–17; 7:11–12, 17–23

Then I remember a sunny afternoon in Canterbury, the day Sir Harry Secombe
and I met God, who told us his version of the story of Noah and the flood. If
it wasn't actually God himself, it was someone very like the traditional image
of the old man in the sky: the late Marius Goring (1912–98), a distinguished
Shakespearean actor, who was playing the Almighty in the mystery plays at
Canterbury Cathedral.

It was the first time that Harry and I had worked together, and my first
experience of his natural and easy-going approach to interviews, which he
called his 'chats'. This approach made his appearances on *Songs of Praise* so
welcome later on. Harry always wanted his *Highway* guests to be the stars of
the show, and people were so happy to meet and talk to such a well-loved

figure that he only ever needed to ask one or two brief, prompting questions to bring out their stories of faith.

On this afternoon, 'God' had a lot to tell us, and there was no need or opportunity for Harry to speak at all. We were in Canterbury for an Advent edition of ITV's *Highway*, and Harry wanted to know what playing the ultimate role was like for Marius. Neither of us was quite ready for what followed, and I think this was the only time when a *Highway* interview began and ended without Harry once having the chance to open his mouth

– except, perhaps, for when he met and interviewed his old friend and arch-rival from *Songs of Praise*, the late Dame Thora Hird.

We never found out anything about Marius, but for a few moments, it was as if a little window had opened into the actor's mind, and we really almost seemed to meet God. First, we saw the colossal costume in which 'God the Creator' appeared. It was the colour of stone, which allowed 'God' to melt into the architecture of Canterbury Cathedral like an ancient sculpture, motionless and unnoticed by the audience until speaking his first words, when everyone jumped out of their skins.

Rushing on with flamboyant gestures, Marius began enthusiastically describing his favourite scene in the play to a bemused Harry – the story of Noah and the flood:

God is absolutely fed up with mankind, see, and he's decided to get rid of the lot. But then he thinks, 'I'll give mankind one more chance through Noah.'

So it all comes to Noah in a vision or a dream, and he gets his instructions from God to build the ark. Then Noah thinks, 'Hang on a minute! There's an old shipwright friend of mine who could help. I'll ask him how to do it.'

So this man appears and gives him all the technical advice. And he says, 'Now look, Noee, build it 300 cubits in length, 50 in breadth – to give it strength. This is how to measure up. And now don't forget, or it will all go wrong.' And he walks off.

So the animals all come in, and when the flood is all over, Noah looks out of the window, and suddenly his old friend is back again. And before he thinks to wonder, how ever did he get here, cos he ought to have been drowned with everybody else, the old friend says, 'Noee, Noee, I tell you what, let's have a rainbow, shall we? Just to celebrate, you and God, that you understand one another, and never let's have this horrible thing happen again, shall we?' And then the old friend says, 'Well, my blessing now I give here to thee, Noah, and have no more fear, my vengeance thou need not fear – and now farewell, my darlin' dear!' And he walks off.

And suddenly Noah realises, 'Good heavens, I've been talking to God and I didn't know it!'

And with that, Marius gave Harry a big kiss and walked off too, and we never saw him again. God bless you too, old friends, Harry and Marius.

Next morning in Slovenia, the storm has passed, and in the sky above, as well as reflected in the water of Lake Bled, I see the finest double rainbow of my life.

My bow I set in the clouds
to be a sign of the covenant
between myself and the earth.
When I bring clouds over the earth,
the rainbow will appear in the clouds.

Then I shall remember the covenant which I have made with you and with all living creatures, and never again will the waters become a flood to destroy all creation.
GENESIS 9:13–15

CHRISTMAS

Nativity (15th century) attributed to Paolo Schiavo (1387–after 1462).

chapter nine

Christingle

· · · · · · · · · · · · · · ·

A<small>ND IT CAME TO PASS</small> in those days, that there went out a decree from Caesar Augustus, that all the world should be taxed. (And this taxing was first made when Cyrenius was Governor of Syria.) And all went to be taxed, every one into his own city. And Joseph also went up from Galilee, out of the city of Nazareth, into Judea, unto the city of David, which is called Bethlehem; (because he was of the house and lineage of David:) To be taxed with Mary his espoused wife, being great with child. And so it was, that, while they were there, the days were accomplished that she should be delivered. And she brought forth her firstborn son, and wrapped him in swaddling clothes, and laid him in a manger; because there was no room for them in the inn.

LUKE 2:1–7

F<small>our</small>-year-old Anna and her little sister, Kirstie, are getting ready for their first Christingle service. Their parents, Sara and Alasdair, and their grandparents, who have arrived for the family Christmas, are in on the preparations too. Two large, fresh oranges have been chosen, red ribbon has been plundered from the dressmaking box, and eight cocktail sticks, four for each orange, have been loaded with raisins and glacé fruits.

Finally, a small candle has been pressed into the top of each ripe orange. This is a Christingle.

In our village in Midlothian, Christians of all denominations, and some who don't belong to any one in particular, join together on Christmas Eve for an annual service of carols, where each of us will be given a Christingle to hold. The Church of Scotland minister stands next to the Roman Catholic priest to preside. The local school has made enough Christingles for all. Our oranges are our home-made symbols of the earth God created, who, as the song goes, has 'got the whole world in his hand'.

The Christingle service appears to have originated in the Moravian Church, which grew out of the Bohemian Brethren in the 15th century in what is now Eastern Europe. The Moravian Christians were pledged to a life of poverty, aiming to realise the ideals of the Sermon on the Mount. One of its members was John Cennick (1718–55), who became a friend of John and Charles Wesley, but was perhaps more gifted as a teacher and preacher than as a hymn-writer. His words, 'Lo! He cometh, endless trumpets blow before his bloody sign!' were thankfully altered by Charles Wesley to 'Lo! He comes with clouds descending.'

The Moravian Church, with its emphasis on fundamental evangelical Christianity, has a strong appeal in the USA, and it is from there that the idea of a Christingle service has travelled back to Europe.

Now everyone has assembled in the parish kirk of Cranstoun. Beside the communion table are the rows and rows of beautifully prepared Christingles. As darkness falls outside, we listen to the Bible reading and sing a carol that tells the story of the Christingle:

It's rounded like an orange,
* this earth on which we stand;*
and we praise the God who holds it
* in the hollow of his hand.*

A candle, burning brightly,
can cheer the darkest night
and these candles tell how Jesus
came to bring a dark world light.

The ribbon round the orange
reminds us of the cost;
how the Shepherd, strong and gentle,
gave his life to save the lost.

Four seasons with their harvest
supply the food we need,
and the Spirit gives a harvest
that can make us rich indeed.

We come with our Christingles
to tell of Jesus' birth
and we praise the God who blessed us
by his coming to this earth.

So Father, we would thank you
for all that you have done,
and for all that you have given us
through the coming of your Son.

'CHRISTINGLE CAROL' BY BASIL BRIDGE (b. 1927);
SUNG TO THE TUNE OF 'THE HOLLY AND THE IVY'

Then the time comes to light the candles, and we follow the children out of the pews to collect the Christingles, each with its candle now burning brightly. We walk in procession out through the doors, all round the church, and back inside again. The congregation has overruled the minister's protest that he cannot see in the dark and has turned out all the lights. We sing the last carol and say our prayers by the light of our Christingles. Sitting near us in a wheelchair is an old lady, bright-eyed with happiness in the candlelight as she holds her orange in arthritic hands and looks at it in amazed wonder.

Back at home with their Christingles, Anna and Kirstie gravely examine the tempting pieces of fruit attached to their oranges. Anna leans forward to blow out her candle and make a wish, for 'Didn't you say it's a birthday party?'

But when the hour of delivery was come, about midnight of the Lord's day, Mary raised herself up and supported herself against a post that happened to be there; but Joseph remained seated, sad within himself, pondering perhaps on the hopelessness of procuring such things as were necessary. But at length he too arose, and put some hay in the manger, and strewed some at the feet of the Virgin and then drew apart once more; and it was then that the Son of God issued from his mother's womb… and immediately the mother leaned over him, raised him up and embraced him, overcome by a sweet love; and she pressed him to her breast, then wrapped him in the veil from her head and laid him in the manger. Then the ox and the ass, bending their knees, put their muzzles over the side of the manger and breathed on the Child, as if they understood that a child so poorly clad, in such a cold place, had need of being warmed. And then the mother, having kneeled, prayed and said, rendering thanks to God:

'I thank thee, Lord and Father, that thou hast given me thy Son, and I beseech thee, Eternal Father, and thou the living God, who art my Son.'

Joseph in his turn worshipped the Child in the same way, and then he took the saddle off the ass and unstrapped the woollen cushion and placed it near the manger, so that Mary could lie down there; and Mary lay down on this cushion and placed the saddle under her elbow; and thus she stayed, the mistress of the world, keeping her eyes fixed on the cradle with all her heart turned towards her cherished Son…

'THE BIRTH OF JESUS', FROM *MEDITATIONES VITAE CHRISTI* (c. 1270), COMPOSED BY
A FRIAR MINOR FOR A POOR CLARE, AND OFTEN ATTRIBUTED TO ST BONAVENTURE

On the Way to Bethlehem with an Old Piano

● ● ● ● ● ● ● ● ● ● ● ● ●

As far as music goes, I've been very fortunate. Perhaps never more so than when the previous occupants of the flat we moved into when I was a child couldn't manage to remove their piano. As soon as I managed to climb up onto the stool, this neglected, out-of-tune upright became my entry to the magic garden. Where does the gift of music come from? I think it must be part of the mystery of the genes.

JOHN RUTTER (b. 1945)

John Rutter and I first met in the 1970s, when we worked together to make *Songs of Praise* from Clare College for Advent 1977. Since then, he has become famous, partly for being the composer of some of the nation's most popular Christmas carols. Thirty years on, we have met again, and John is trying hard to answer the sort of question that television producers always ask artists.

When I first began working in religious broadcasting, the late Malcolm Muggeridge advised me, 'Dear boy, you don't seriously think that they can

answer the question with words? Just use your eyes and ears to understand.'
But 30 years on, I find I still want to ask the question: where does a composer
find his inspiration?

Surprisingly, in view of his work composing and conducting Christian
music, John says that he is an agnostic. 'However, I do think the church
shaped me, and I realise how much I owe it still. The church didn't make a
chorister of me, but it did make a friend and supporter of me.' Not many, I
suspect, required to go to chapel every day at school, become quite such a
friend and supporter. From the age of 17, John was writing carols, and at
just 21, he was responsible for a full album of music.

It had begun with failure, when he was still at school:

*The first carol I wrote, I called the 'Nativity Carol' and sent it into the annual Bach
Choir Carol Competition. I didn't mean to steal it, but I think I may have got the
theme from one of Elgar's* Enigma Variations. *Anyway, I hadn't read the rules of the
competition properly, which required that the winning carol must contain a refrain
that could be sung by the whole audience in the Albert Hall. So I hadn't a chance
with the 'Nativity Carol' and it was put away in a drawer for years and forgotten.*

When he was in his second year of reading music at Clare College, Cambridge,
John was asked to put on a concert that December, and he decided it would
be good to finish off with some carols. 'I remembered the carol in the drawer,
and as well as arranging some traditional ones, I wrote the "Shepherd's
Pipe Carol". Then I prepared for what I thought would be the first and last
performance.'

The original inspiration for the 'Shepherd's Pipe Carol' came from a
book of Picasso reproductions, among which was an early watercolour of a
little shepherd boy:

*He looked no more than seven or eight years old, and he had his arm round a
little woolly lamb, and I found it enchanting. It looked almost like a life study.*

I began to wonder about the boy – was he musical, and, if so, what instrument would he play? Where was he going and what was his story?

The carol also emerged from an experience from his school days, when he had taken the lead role in a local church performance of *Amahl and the Night Visitors*, Gian Carlo Menotti's opera about a poor, lame, pipe-playing shepherd boy named Amahl, who goes to Bethlehem.

The two things came together and began to coalesce when I found I had a little phrase going round and round in my head: 'On the way to Bethlehem'.

Composition for me is a compulsion. I dread it at first. I sit in front of the empty page, and it is only the very distant prospect of the tingle you get when the composer becomes the conductor and raises his baton for the first performance that keeps me going.

The Little Shepherd by Pablo Picasso (1882–1973).

Living as he does on the edge of the Fens, with all their meteorologically induced moods, John uses a familiar journey to explain the artistic process – something I can really understand:

As you drive across the Fens to Ely Cathedral on a misty day, you can see nothing.
Then there is a distant, looming outline, without even the slightest detail. Then, as
you get closer, you begin to make out individual features, and finally, arriving at the
west door of the cathedral, every precise detail is clear.

Going through the hills on a night all starry,
    on the way to Bethlehem,
far away I heard a shepherd boy piping,
    on the way to Bethlehem.
Angels brought this message:
    dance and sing for joy that Christ the King is
come to bring us peace on earth, and he's lying
    cradled there at Bethlehem.

Tell me, shepherd boy piping tunes so merrily,
    on the way to Bethlehem,
who will hear your tunes on these hills so lonely,
    on the way to Bethlehem?
Angels brought this message:
    dance and sing for joy that Christ the King is
come to bring us peace on earth, and he's lying
    cradled there at Bethlehem.

None may hear my pipes on these hills so lonely,
    on the way to Bethlehem;
but a King will hear me play sweet lullabies,
    when I get to Bethlehem.
Angels in the sky
    hovered o'er the manger where the babe was lying
cradled in the arms of his mother Mary.
    sleeping now at Bethlehem.

Where is this new King, shepherd boy piping merrily,
is he there at Bethlehem?
I will find him soon by the star shining brightly
in the sky o'er Bethlehem.
Angels in the sky brought this message nigh:
dance and sing for joy that Christ the King is
come to bring us peace on the earth,
and he's lying, cradled there at Bethlehem.

May I come with you, shepherd boy piping merrily,
come with you to Bethlehem?
Pay my homage too at the new King's cradle,
is it far to Bethlehem?
Angels in the sky brought this message nigh:
dance and sing for joy that Christ the infant King is
born this night in lowly stable yonder,
born for you at Bethlehem.

'SHEPHERD'S PIPE CAROL' BY JOHN RUTTER (b. 1945)

Time Travellers in
the Cathedral

• • • • • • • • • • • • • •

chapter eleven

I LOOKED AND SAW THIS FANTASTIC SIGHT – the
floodlit cathedral, gorgeous, stunning, out of
this world, certainly out of any world I'd been
inhabiting. It was radiant, ravishing. I stopped
dead and that was the moment when the
scales fell from my eyes. I felt that I had been
presented with some extraordinary gift. I
could see and recognise the overpowering
beauty of that cathedral – which was the sign
pointing beyond itself to the reality which
was still hidden from my conscious mind.

SUSAN HOWATCH (b. 1940)

Standing in the garden of an old house in Cathedral Close in
Salisbury on a winter's evening, I am looking across at the view of
the cathedral described by Susan Howatch. I may even be looking
from exactly the same vantage point, for many of the fictional events
in her famous *Starbridge* series, which are based on actual events in the
history of the Church of England, are set in this close, where the novelist
made her home. Others too have been inspired and moved by this most
beautiful of medieval cathedrals.

As the light fades on this December afternoon, homeward-bound drivers edging their way through traffic around the southern fringe of the city may catch brief glimpses of the great medieval spire that inspired the artist, John Constable. From where I stand, looking across the darkening garden, the massive building appears to be floating on translucent light. Hugh Dickinson, a former dean, described the cathedral as light, elegant and full of slender detail, and he was reminded of the spacecraft in *Star Wars*®, journeying across vast galaxies. It is the perfect setting for *Songs of Praise*, for tonight, the space-age technology of the third millennium has

come to Salisbury Cathedral. With almost 1,000 singers from all around Wiltshire, there is to be the experience normally reserved for science fiction: a little time travelling. Although Advent has scarcely begun, tonight the cathedral is decorated for 25 December, and the singers have come to sing carols for a television recording of *Songs of Praise* for Christmas.

Even after more than 30 years of making television programmes, there is something about an evening like this that still excites me. The building itself will be enough to beguile the director, Pamela Hossick, as she looks

through her six or seven cameras dotted around the cathedral, and the presence of the lights and the cameras may be what makes it an occasion for many of the participants. But for me, it is something different. What I can't wait for is the feeling of belonging that you experience on a big *Songs of Praise*, when hundreds of singers come together, and in a few hours become one voice. Hurrying across the close with my small, unreliable torch, towards the serried ranks of television lights illuminating the cathedral's west end, I insist on taking a short cut across the playing fields, and almost at once my wife and I have stumbled into the 'slough of despond' in the shape of a big, muddy patch.

'O God, you are to be praised with the sound of trumpet and the voice of the angels; help us now to join our music with the music of heaven.'

Standing at the head of a large, anxious-looking choir in the nave, the cathedral's precentor, Jeremy Davies, prays before we sing the first carol. He has popped in to welcome the congregation, sort out any urgent problems and warn them of what he calls a 'bitty' evening ahead.

This is perhaps the moment to thank God for Sydney Evans, another of Salisbury Cathedral's former deans, who, although no sci-fi enthusiast, was the first to allow television cameras in to record the cathedral's own Advent carol service, which begins by the light of one candle. When Chris Mann, one of the BBC's most inspired directors, first approached him in 1981, the dean had visions of the choir being mown down in the dark by tank-sized cameras. But Chris was never one to be easily dissuaded. In 1982, a single cameraman and Chris, both dressed from head to foot in black, were permitted to record the service on video. As the candlelight slowly spread throughout the cathedral, the result was, in Chris's word, 'Magic!'

Sydney was won over, sort of, and the following year, Chris was back with a full outside-broadcast unit, also arrayed in black. Before the recording of the service began, I stood at the back with Angela Tilby, then a television producer and now vice-principal of Westcott House Theological College in Cambridge. What on earth, we wondered, were the cameras going to see? Apart from the luminous screen of a camera viewfinder, we ourselves could see nothing.

We should have had more faith – in Chris. As the candlelight spread, it became apparent that this unstoppable director had somehow persuaded Salisbury's dean to turn a blind eye to a dozen dustbin-like devices, each containing television lights on dimmers, concealed among the congregation. It was a conjuring trick, a cheat, of course, but the numinous experience of an ancient cathedral's traditional worship by candlelight was caught live on television for the first time.

Tonight, in full fig, splendid in their gold vestments, all the principal cathedral clergy have come, led by June Osborne, the acting dean. The uniformed first-aid volunteers of the St John's Ambulance Brigade (St Andrew's in Scotland) are also there, as they are for every *Songs of Praise* recording. They are a reassuring presence, for long rehearsals can prove quite an endurance test. Glynn Reeve has served 43 years with the brigade, and she is accompanied by Stacey Wood, who joined only four months ago. Although remaining behind the scenes, both are just as eager to join in the singing as the people who have managed to get seats in the front rows.

All eyes are drawn to an enormous nativity tableau at the centre crossing, where a nave altar would normally be, around which the cathedral choir of boys and men as well as Britain's first cathedral girls' choir assemble for part of the cathedral's own annual climax to Christmas. On a mountain of straw are all the traditional figures around the crib: the holy family, ox and ass, shepherds and wise men – and also a little cat, a reminder of the moment in a previous year when a real cat was found sleeping peacefully by the manger. Under the television lights, gigantic angelic figures suspended above look translucent and ethereal. It is hard to believe that artist Peter Rush crafted the whole scene from papier mâché and the plastic bags of a well-known supermarket chain.

Suddenly, the waiting is over, and the strange alchemy that I always look forward to begins. We are all being transformed, even me, a virtual non-singer, into a choir of angels. We are coaxed and cajoled into making the sound of music that should see us safely across the River Jordan. At least, that is how it feels, but, as anyone who has ever taken part in *Songs of Praise* knows, we shall probably have to do it all again.

For the grand finale, the cathedral choirs complete a manoeuvre that might have defeated the famous 1930s' Hollywood choreographer, Busby Berkely. Without a word of command, while singing 'In the bleak mid-winter', the choirs form two concentric circles moving in opposite directions around the nativity tableau. Pamela, the director, has positioned a remote camera on a long arm high above, to look down on them and see perfect symmetry in motion. Or not, if it goes wrong.

The moment arrives, watched closely by presenter Pam Rhodes, resplendent in Santa Claus red. Tonight, it is not just Salisbury Cathedral as 'a living, moody personality', in Susan Howatch's words, that makes the magic but all creation. Into the middle of the circling choirs moves David Stancliffe, bishop of Salisbury, with his acolytes, in solemn procession down from the high altar, to kneel at the crib, while a treble from the choir finds his way among the magi to sing the solo verse:

What can I give him,
poor as I am?
If I were a shepherd,
I would bring a lamb;
if I were a wise man,
I would do my part;
yet what I can I give him –
give my heart.
CHRISTINA ROSSETTI (1830–94)

Almost before the last note of the final carol, 'Hark! the herald angels sing', has died away, the cathedral's vergers are hard at work, taking out all the Christmas decorations. Next evening, believe it or not, the choirs and television cameras will be back in Salisbury Cathedral, to record a programme for the following Lent. But that's another story.

chapter twelve

Sidney Goes
to the Manger

●●●●●●●●●●●●●●●

NOW IN THIS SAME DISTRICT there were shepherds
out in the fields, keeping watch through the night
over their flock. Suddenly an angel of the Lord
appeared to them, and the glory of the Lord shone
round them. They were terrified, but the angel
said, 'Do not be afraid; I bring you good news,
news of great joy for the whole nation. Today
there has been born to you in the city of David
a deliverer – the Messiah, the Lord. This will be
the sign for you: you will find a baby wrapped
in swaddling clothes and lying in a manger.'

LUKE 2:8–12

*I had no feeling of anxiety, only a sense of exultation, as I heard the bells ring
out above the roaring of the gale. Never at any other time have I been so
conscious of the wonder of the world. Over the high altar burned a white
light proclaiming the presence of the incarnate God, whose nativity we were
celebrating, while above our heads was another light, burning red, warning the
players that any sounds within the church were at that moment being transmitted
over the face of the earth.*

FROM *THIRTY YEARS AT ST HILARY* (1935) BY BERNARD WALKE

Bernard Walke, vicar of a tiny parish in western Cornwall, was describing one Christmas Eve in the 1920s. Surrounded by the familiar faces of his congregation in the candlelight, he was used to hearing to the nativity play he had written coming to life in rich Cornish voices, carol singing and bell-ringing. This night was different, however, because unseen hundreds and thousands were also listening as the story unfolded, but without moving from their own firesides. The BBC had come to St Hilary's, and St Hilary's was broadcasting its nativity play to the world.

Father Bernard was an extraordinary Anglican priest. He has been described as both deeply traditional and yet ahead of his time. As a man, he was both deeply caring and profoundly awkward. He took on everyone who stood in the way of reviving the spiritual life of his community in Cornwall, and not uniquely in the history of the church, he was frequently on a collision course with the ecclesiastical authorities.

He drew many artists and poets to his remote little church of St Hilary. Even the equally awkward George Bernard Shaw came once. Among them was a radio producer from the BBC at Savoy Hill in London. Filson Young was an imaginative and opinionated member of Sir John Reith's team, and his forthright views frequently infuriated the BBC's first director general. He was fascinated by the potential of radio to stimulate the imagination, and he believed that programmes were best listened to in the dark. To him, religion as a full-blooded experience was a more fertile area for broadcasting than for a sermon at the microphone. A chance meeting with Father Bernard introduced him to the tiny, remote Cornish community where nobody had a radio, but which he could see offered all that he needed to tell the Christmas story on air as it had never been told before. For the next 10 years, Bernard's play, *Bethlehem*, directed by Filson, was to be the high point of Christmas Eve for BBC radio audiences.

Sidney Hayes first took part in the *Bethlehem* broadcast in 1929, before an audience that included Sir John Reith and Ramsey MacDonald, the prime minister. Now 83, Sidney has lived for most of his life in the parish of St Hilary, where he joined the 'surpliced' church choir at the age of nine. He recalls:

The BBC officials were astounded that they got such a response because of us. We were just country folk, village folk, that was all we were. But we thought it was marvellous to be able to broadcast to the nation.

In those days, the church was all decorated with lots of branches, all covered with tinsel. There was a man down the lane who used to build a marvellous crib, and the angel Gabriel, she was very good, she lived across from the church in the farm, so she didn't have far to come.

The BBC, on the other hand, did:

The actors rehearse for the BBC radio broadcast of Father Bernard's play, *Bethlehem*, sometime between 1929 and 1931.

They had to run a cable across the fields from a temporary telephone somewhere in the village. There were horses and cows out in the fields too, so we expected any time that they would chew through the cable.

We didn't have electricity in the church, so the BBC had to bring masses of big batteries, which filled one of the side chapels. They had three microphones, with one near our shepherds' encampment, which was actually up in the belfry.

I was a shepherd boy the first time. We had all learned our lines. Father Bernard didn't allow us to have scripts, and as each scene went on, Filson Young came over in case we needed a prompt – which we never did. We knew we had got to get it exactly right.

We all knew Filson Young. He was a very good organist, and in our village where there was only one car, we all used to see him arrive at the vicarage in his very old, silver-coloured AC6.

Bethlehem was revived in the 1990s, with Sidney taking a principal role, but it couldn't have made the same impact as in the 1920s. Church worship was very formal in those days, and the very idea of any sort of drama was almost unheard of. It must have raised the eyebrows of many church dignitaries of the time. As Sidney recalls: 'There were six or eight children with bells strapped to their ankles and sticks to beat the floor, just like Morris dancers, and we had a man who played the violin as they did a dance in front of the crib.'

Drawing on folk traditions with an atmosphere of deeply felt devotion to the nativity not only made Father Bernard a revolutionary in his church but also made revolutionary radio. Rarely before had amateur performers spoken on the BBC, and certainly not without reading a script scrutinised and approved by Savoy Hill.

Unfortunately, early broadcasting could arouse heated opinions, good or bad, as much as it does today, and in 1932, the Kensites, a sect who saw the nativity play and Bernard's vision as idolatrous, attacked and desecrated St Hilary's Church. In 1936, Bernard left the village, suffering from ill-health. The broadcasts were over.

Sidney and his wife, who nowadays never miss *Songs of Praise*, can look out across the fields to the woods that still shelter St Hilary's from winter gales. Sidney is proud of his days as a 'celebrity' on the radio. Over the years, he went from being 'a simple boy' to 'second shepherd'. He showed me a faded photograph of a rehearsal in the vicarage. There at the back is Sidney, a small boy in the choir. He and his friends used to walk home after evensong across moonlit fields, singing all the hymns and carols they could remember. He reminisces:

Most of the people who were in the play, well, they're gone on now. Mrs Peters, who played the mother of the holy family, she was a good singer, as was her husband, Nicky, who was one of the shepherds, with Tom Rowe, Willy Curnow and myself. I'm the last one now.

One thing I'm sorry about: we never did have a donkey in the play, although Father Bernard, who loved animals, did keep them. We boys used to ride one called Aladdin whenever we could.

Sidney is proud of the autographed copy of the play given to him by Father Bernard. Here are his last lines as the second shepherd, addressed to the holy family at the crib:

We must be getting on now and look after the sheep. They're bound to get teasy, for they'll be wanting fresh pasture at the coming of the day.

Zacky, Jacob, boy and all, take your hats off and down on your two knees and say goodbye.

Goodbye, kind Joseph. Goodbye, Mary dear, and the holy infant in the manger there.

Goodbye all; God bless 'e, my dears.

While shepherds watched their flocks
    by night,
  all seated on the ground,
the angel of the Lord came down,
  and glory shone around.

'Fear not,' said he (for mighty dread
  had seized their troubled mind),
'glad tidings of great joy I bring
  to you and all mankind.

'To you in David's town this day
  is born of David's line
a Saviour, who is Christ the Lord;
  and this shall be the sign:

'The heavenly Babe you there shall find
  to human view displayed,
all meanly wrapped in swathing-bands,
  and in a manger laid.'

Thus spake the seraph; and forthwith
  appeared a shining throng
of angels, praising God, who thus
  addressed their joyful song:

'All glory be to God on high,
  and to the world be peace!
Goodwill henceforth from heaven to earth
  begin and never cease!'

NAHUM TATE (1652–1715) (ALTERED)

chapter thirteen

Christmas with the Animals

• • • • • • • • • • • • •

Once in royal David's city
stood a lowly cattle shed,
where a mother laid her baby
in a manger for his bed:
Mary was that mother mild,
Jesus Christ her little child.

CECIL FRANCES ALEXANDER (1818–95)

I love animals, but if I have to watch *Animal Hospital*, it is from behind the sofa. The moment when Rolf Harris says, 'Sadly, little Fluffy didn't make it,' brings back all the grief that followed the death of each of our own beloved animal companions. Eighty-two-year-old Mrs Joan Scott, who appeared on *Songs of Praise* from Selby Abbey, helped me to try to be a little more sensible, a little less sentimental. You may remember her interview, a tour of her Selby Animal Sanctuary. It ended with the faces of the animals – foxes, pigs, owls and a donkey – looking directly at us, and a question from Mrs Scott, 'When you look into those faces, you couldn't not believe, could you?' This led into the hymn setting of Mary's song, the Magnificat: 'Tell out, my soul, the greatness of the Lord'.

To my mind, this is *Songs of Praise* at its best, when someone appears, albeit briefly, and out of their own experience gives you a new thought to go with a familiar hymn. The words of Mary's song celebrate the upside-down world of the kingdom of God, where the meek inherit the earth and the poor are filled with good things, while the rich are sent away empty. And it was surrounded by animals, ox, ass and sheep, in a Bethlehem stable that Mary's Son was soon to be born. So surely the animals have something to tell us about the kingdom of God?

After watching the Selby programme, I just had to go and meet Mrs Scott and see for myself. Mrs Scott shares almost every waking moment with the creatures of the Selby Animal Sanctuary. She certainly believes the animals have things to teach us, and she always looks forward to Christmas, when she can remind visitors of the old legend of why every donkey has a distinctive cross on its back – to show the world their humble but important part in the story of Jesus. She likes to imagine her animals kneeling down at midnight on Christmas Eve, because they were the first witnesses, even before the shepherds, of the birth in Bethlehem.

'I don't go and look,' she says. 'That's something for them, and not for me.'

Christmas Eve, and twelve of the clock.
  'Now they are all on their knees,'
an elder said as we sat in a flock
  by the embers in hearthside ease.

We pictured the meek mild creatures where
  they dwelt in their strawy pen,
nor did it occur to one of us there
  to doubt they were kneeling then.

So fair a fancy few would weave
  in these years! Yet, I feel,
if someone said on Christmas Eve,
  'Come; see the oxen kneel,

'In the lonely barton by yonder coomb
    our childhood used to know,'
I should go with him in the gloom,
    hoping it might be so.
'THE OXEN' BY THOMAS HARDY (1840–1928)

Whatever goes on in the animal kingdom on Christmas Eve, it is business as usual on Christmas morning in the Selby Animal Sanctuary. Even though she's in her eighties, Mrs Scott is up at 6.15 a.m. and soon chopping up apples and carrots for the donkeys, pouring out pellets for Piggy, the Vietnamese pot-bellied pig, and coarse mix and sugar beet for Molly, the blind sheep. Then, regardless of the weather, she is down at the huge pond feeding resident and visiting ducks. Next, it is back to the many sheds and runs for 'the inevitable mucking out, because they must all have clean water and beds every day'. Even hibernating hedgehogs have fresh food and water every day. 'Sometimes they wake up because they're not warm enough, so you put a little handful of fresh bedding out for them, just in case.'

She told me, 'I think I'm one of the luckiest people in the world,' as we sat in the converted portacabin that has been her home for almost 12 years. After her husband, Tommy, died, she sold her bungalow to raise money for the sanctuary. 'He would have done the same. I'm not a martyr; it is what I thought was right, and you know, if it is not right, it won't happen.' I notice a plaque on her wall, which reads, 'Dull women have immaculate houses.'

As we sit, sharing our chairs with Rover and Cassie, two dogs who are keeping a close eye on me, Badger, a 'new' old cat, peers through a glass door at the strange visitor. It is quite a scrum today.

People come here every day, sometimes even on Christmas Day, wanting rid of their pets, but I can only take in the sick and injured now.

Often, I have owls and hedgehogs in here too, if they're injured, and they have to find a seat where I can keep my eye on them. All animals want love, and you don't sort of love them one minute and push them away the next. You must love each animal for itself. They're not people, but they do all have different needs.

We go outside so that I can meet barn owls and tawny owls and then Foxy, a beautiful arctic fox. 'I wasn't going to give him a posh name, because he'd get above himself, but we had to be taught what to do to make him happy.' Foxy obviously has great communication skills. I survey a huge range of huts and runs, which are now his home; certainly a posh-fox residence.

Before my visit ends, there is a moment to meet the donkeys, the

crosses on their backs now covered by smart New Zealand coats, and to hear a sad postscript to the *Songs of Praise* interview. Just a week after transmission of the Selby programme in 2002, Marigold, one of its stars, died, leaving Bridget, who also appeared on the programme, on her own. Marigold now rests at peace under a newly planted rowan tree. Now Chrissie has arrived and is learning to live in harmony with Bridget, an ancient black sheep and a big duck, appropriately named Sir Francis Drake, who came to the sanctuary after a dog had attacked him.

I'm not angry with God when they die. It doesn't get easier, but you get to understand more. I'm not very profound, but I'm sure that I'm here to be of service to the animals. And you can't believe what they give me. It is peace beyond words. God is concerned not with what we want but what we need. If I've got enough food and enough to feed the animals, and we're all warm, that's all that matters. And I think I will be reunited with them one day. They won't need me, and I won't need them, but I will be glad to see them, if you know what I mean.

I felt that in Selby Animal Sanctuary, I too had a glimpse of the kingdom of God.

After the very bright light,
and the talking bird,
and the singing,
and the sky filled up wi' wings,
and then the silence,

Our lads sez
We'd better go, then.
Stay, Shep. Good dog, stay.
So I stayed wi' t' sheep.

After they cum back,
it sounded grand, what they'd seen:
camels, and kings, and such,
wi' presents – human sort,
not the kind you eat –
and a baby. Presents wes for him.
Our lads took him a lamb.

I had to stay behind wi' t' sheep.
Pity they didn't tek me along too.
I'm good wi' lambs,
and the baby might have liked a dog
after all that myrrh and such.
'THE SHEEPDOG' BY U.A. FANTHORPE (b. 1929)

chapter fourteen

Star Wars® in St Mary's

> CHILD, FOR US SINNERS
> poor and in the manger,
> fain we embrace thee, with awe and love;
> who would not love thee,
> loving us so dearly?
> O come, let us adore him,
> O come, let us adore him,
> O come, let us adore him, Christ
> the Lord!

FROM 'O COME, ALL YE FAITHFUL', LATIN (18TH CENTURY),
TRANSLATED BY FREDERICK OAKLEY (1802–80)

There is a terrific hubbub in St Mary's Cathedral, Edinburgh, on Christmas Eve, and all the ingredients for chaos: television cameras being wheeled around, trailing long cables; lights and microphones being adjusted; candles being lit; and 500 overexcited primary-school children arriving and scrambling for seats in the nave. To add to the confusion, there is a supply of electric torches, whose proper purpose will not be revealed until much later; meanwhile they make perfect light sabres in the darkened cathedral for mock *Star Wars*® duels with Darth Vader.

Everyone has arrived now, and here we will stay until a complete Christmas Eve television programme of carols and readings has been recorded for BBC Scotland. As the children's noise crescendoes, it seems incredible not only that order will ever be restored, but that a television programme will emerge from all this, to give joy and pleasure to more than a third of Scotland's viewing audience. In the third millennium since the birth of Jesus, we are offered so much else to beguile us on so many competing television channels that it is good to know that at this time of year, many still turn to the church, even the 'church of the air', to discover again the magic of Christmas.

Matthew Owens, the tall master of the music in Scotland's largest church, is standing on a box, and beside him, on the ground, is the diminutive figure of Christopher Bell, conductor of the National Youth Children's Choir of Scotland. But who is going to create order out of this juvenile mayhem?

'Silence!' Christopher does not shout, but chants the instruction in a sing-song voice.

'Silence!' chorus back 500 voices.

'Listening?' calls the conductor.

'Listening!' sing back the rabble, who have transformed into a choir of angels. Unfortunately, these particular angels cannot fit on the seats, let alone balance on the proverbial pinhead.

'It should be four small people on three adult seats,' says Christopher. 'So squeeze!' Satisfaction. But a few rebellious torches are still seen flickering.

'Put them down on the floor. Do it now!' One hundred per cent satisfaction is achieved. Now we can begin.

Christopher has an international reputation as a conductor. He has the gift of making everyone in his young choirs sing like a bird, and wit and repartee play a big part in his method. Every one of the 500 children here tonight is paying absolute attention now. They have already learned by heart the notes and words of eight carols. But there are some grown-ups here too, and adults always need a carol sheet.

'Parents and supporters,' announces Christopher kindly, but without music in his voice, 'we love you dearly, but the BBC doesn't want viewers to know you are here. So grown-ups must go into hiding.'

Once the adults are settled in the dark in the choir transept, it is Matthew Owens who steps forward to conduct the cathedral choir, St Mary's School orchestra and the huge primary-school choir in the nave in singing 'Once in royal David's city'.

They are word and note perfect, but the cameras still need sorting out.

'Sit down, take the weight off your brain,' sings out Christopher. 'This is what it is to be professional: we'll do it again and again until it is right.'

Behind a pillar near the front, 11-year-old Amy Moar must have the most professional approach to what turns into a very long three hours. Amy loves every moment. I can see that she is enjoying the experience, but Amy cannot see me because she has been blind from birth. Her mother, Anne, watches the conductor's beat and taps it out with her fingers on Amy's open hands. I learn two more facts about Amy as the carols and readings are successfully recorded, one by one. She has been playing the piano since she was three, and

neither her blindness nor a kidney transplant has in any way dulled her enthusiasm for life. She always gives her all.

A few days later, when Christmas finally arrived, and the same cathedral was full to overflowing for midnight mass, Graham Forbes, the provost, compared God's risk in the incarnation with 'risk' as understood by the world of life insurance.

Our world is small, fragile and vulnerable, just like the child in the manger. Any reasonable risk assessor would say that the divine strategy of self-giving love is far too risky. No insurance company I know would touch it with a bargepole. It is founded not on strength, on thunderbolts that zap enemies, but on fragility, on a helpless child in a manger, a helpless man on a cross, on disciples who, like Peter, deny,

or who, like Judas, betray. Folk like you, folk like me. That's the way of divine love…
The Christ, who seeks to be born in us this night, seeks us to join him in the risk of
divine love, to work to build up his kingdom of justice and peace.

Risky? Absolutely. True? I believe so.

That was something Amy would understand.

Now the moment everyone has been waiting for arrives, as Christopher
again sings out, 'Listening?' and back comes the angel chorus: 'Listening!'

'Switch on your torches, shine them upwards and keep absolutely still.'

Then they sing 'Silent Night' very, *very*, gently:

Silent night, holy night!
Son of God, O how bright
love is smiling from thy face…

What the shining, upturned faces won't
see until they watch the programme on
Christmas Eve is that Jim Hunter, the
television director, has put a 'star' filter on
each camera lens; the torches have become
500 little stars, and reflected off the cathedral roof are 500 little stars shining
back. Then Scotland's youngest television presenters, secondary-school pupils
Sarah Wann and Steven McIntosh, wish the audience a very happy Christmas.
And it is all over. With torch batteries flat, and each flaked-out little chorister
rewarded with crisps and cartons of juice, it is time to go home.

'I want to play the big cathedral organ,' Amy announces. Too late – the
hubbub is back, and even the loudest organ will not drown out the sound of
the faithful 500 making their way out into the darkness.

In John Masefield's world of *The Box of Delights*, also set on Christmas
Eve in a cathedral, the music is about to reach a crescendo. Young Kay
Harker, on the train returning home from school for Christmas, finds his cosy

world of buttered eggs and muffins invaded by the forces of darkness and running wolves. Kay must heroically thwart the evil wizard, Abner Brown, alias Dr Bottledale of the Missionary College, and his sinister underlings, Foxy and Chubby, also cunningly disguised as clergymen. He must free the real bishop, the dean and the entire choir of Tatchester Cathedral, who are all trapped under the icy weir of a water mill, their lives ransomed for the magical Box of Delights, with its elixir of eternal life. In the nick of time, and with the aid of the forces of light, an old magician named Cole Hawlings and his Barney dog, Toby, everyone is freed, and now they all rush back to the cathedral for the midnight celebration.

Here is how John Keir Cross's classic *Children's Hour* broadcast ends:

THE MUSIC HAS ALMOST IMPERCEPTIBLY CROSS-FADED WITH THE MID-DISTANT EFFECT OF MANY CHURCH BELLS RINGING, CONTINUING BEHIND THE NARRATOR'S (I.E. KAY HARKER'S) VOICE:

Narrator: *And now we were down from the heavens, and skimming over the feathery snow itself, piled high in the narrow lanes after the great storm. All the church bells of all the parishes were ringing – the tremblings of their music went thronging by in the swift air. We saw the great, pinnacled tower of the cathedral, all floodlit for this splendid thousandth night…*

A HUGE, EXCITED CROWD EFFECT HAS BEEN ADDED TO THE BELLS, AND BOTH CONTINUE BEHIND AS WE GO STRAIGHT ON, NOW AT SPEED AGAIN…

… and while the bishop and the choir and all the helpers went hurrying to robe, I saw all the Jones girls, at a great table just outside the cathedral door itself, covered with all sorts of things – and with them was the Barney dog, running as pleased as Punch himself to greet his master.

THE DOG OVERLAPS FROM BEHIND HIM WITH RAPID, APPROACHING BARKING.

Cole Hawlings: *Quiet, quiet, my little lad, on this most blessed night. Of course I'm pleased to see you – I love you very much, and all the wolves are gone at last…*

MUSIC – PERHAPS A MAGNIFICENT ORCHESTRAL VERSION OF 'HARK! THE HERALD-ANGELS SING'. IT SOARS. HOLD FOR AS LONG AS POSSIBLE – THEN DOWN A LITTLE BEHIND THE NARRATOR, NOW VERY CLOSE, AND WITH THE ECHO GONE…

Narrator: *The music shook the whole vast building – it seemed to me, I remember, that it was shaking it to very pieces. All the heads came off all the bodies and moved up into the air. I myself was being shaken to pieces, my own head was coming off, right through the cathedral roof. In fact, the cathedral was no longer there at all, nor any of all that glorious company. No –*

BEHIND, THE MUSIC HAS BEEN CROSS-FADING WITH THE NOISY ARRIVAL OF A TRAIN, JUST DRAWING UP BEHIND HIM WITH A CONTINUING HISS OF STEAM AS HE GOES VIRTUALLY STRAIGHT ON:

Narrator: *– no!… I was in an empty railway carriage on a bitterly cold day, and the train had just drawn in. I was at Condicote Station, with my pocket full of money, just home for the holidays… and… Miss Caroline Louisa was shaking and waking me.*

Miss Caroline: *Why, Kay. Wake up – wake up, my dear! You have been sound asleep! Welcome home, and a merry Christmas. Have you had a nice dream?*

Kay Harker: *[a shade sleepily at first] Oh yes – yes, I have… [then suddenly fully and triumphantly awake] Oh yes – I have! And a merry Christmas to you too, Miss Caroline!*

FROM THE RADIO ADAPTATION BY JOHN KEIR CROSS (1911–67)
OF *THE BOX OF DELIGHTS* (1935) BY JOHN MASEFIELD (1878–1967)

Home Alone

chapter fifteen

IT WAS ALWAYS SAID OF HIM, that he knew
how to keep Christmas well, if any man
alive possessed the knowledge. May that be
truly said of us, and all of us! And so, as
Tiny Tim observed, God bless us, every one!

FROM *A CHRISTMAS CAROL* (1843) BY CHARLES DICKENS (1812–70)

As producer and scriptwriter for the late Dame Thora Hird's *Praise Be!*, my wife, Liz, knew that when Christmas cards began to arrive, it was time to invite the hymn requests for Thora's next series. It was the letters from viewers, talking about their own lives as well as choosing their favourite hymns, that helped Thora touch a deep chord in her *Praise Be!* audience, and just before Christmas was the best time to remind people to write in. Thora would pop round to our flat to be filmed making her annual appeal for viewers to choose their favourite moments from a year of *Songs of Praise*.

It was almost as hush-hush as recording the Queen's Christmas message. In a long morning, Thora made our flat her home; we decorated a tree and surrounded her with Christmas cards, for an appearance all of 15 seconds long. After the recording was finished, the glass of champagne drunk, the cat allowed back into the room, we always said, 'This feels like the real beginning of Christmas.'

Once Thora's trailer had been shown, at the end of the Christmas and New Year *Songs of Praises*, the floodgates would open, with as many as 10,000 requests arriving at the *Praise Be!* office.

Thora died in 2003 at the age of 91, and after a lifetime given to making us laugh and cry, and winning top awards for her remarkable comedy and drama performances, not to mention being the friendly, loving person whom *Praise Be!* viewers felt was their special friend, Thora still had one unfulfilled ambition. She wanted to present her own Christmas Day programme especially for all *Songs of Praise* viewers who were home alone and feeling lonely.

In 17 years of making *Praise Be!*, Thora's postbag overflowed with heart-warming and sometimes heart-rending human stories. In many of the letters, however, there would be one request to which she could not hope to respond. It would go something like this: 'When you're passing, Thora, do pop in for a cup of tea. It would make my day. I'm on my own now, and although everyone around here is very kind, the days seem very long, especially at Christmas.' Even were she as great a tea-lover as her character, Edie, in *Last of the Summer Wine*, Thora would soon have perished in a surfeit of tannin and cucumber sandwiches had she personally accepted all the invitations she received. She could have filled her diary every day for years to come with nothing else but 'popping in'. But why not a special Christmas-morning edition of *Praise Be!*, especially for all those viewers who thought of her as a friend who visited them in their living rooms?

Had she had her wish, I know Thora would have insisted on one request of her own, 'While shepherds watched their flocks by night', sung to the tune 'Lyngham', more familiar to most of us as the tune for Charles Wesley's 'O for a thousand tongues to sing'. But according to Thora, all good Methodists, and especially those brought up within sight and sound of the local Salvation Army band playing on the street corner in Morecambe on Christmas morning, knew this to be the 'right' tune. Shortly before she died following a severe stroke, Thora sang it all the way through from memory, with her daughter, Janette, at her bedside.

Thora's Christmas television special never happened, but on Christmas Day 2002, she made a guest appearance on Radio 2 with Roger Royle, on *Good Morning, Christmas*. For anyone on his or her own, for whom radio is like a best friend, it must have been a happy reunion. It is a great gift, one that Roger and Thora both share, to be able, through television and radio, to make 'you' and 'I' into 'we'.

This rare gift is almost never found in people unaccustomed to broadcasting. But back in the 1980s, it was a television viewer, Bet Busby, who one Christmas morning turned a television audience into 'us'. Every week for over a decade, a different member of the audience provided the home from which the worship programme, *This is the Day*, was broadcast live every Sunday morning. The Bible was read, bread broken, a candle lit, and, above all, the audience shared in the experience of praying for each other through the letters that were read, and for the world through that morning's newspapers.

Christmas Day fell on a Sunday that year, so Bet was the viewer who achieved what Thora never managed, to broadcast live on television on Christmas morning. She shared the presentation with Linda Mary Evans, but Bet herself had an almost unique gift of being able to speak naturally through the impassive lens of a camera, directly to her television-viewing guests.

There was a quiet moment of history made in Bet's first (and I expect last) broadcast. There was a camera in the house next door, where we could see her Muslim neighbour, Mrs Begum, and her children watching the programme on their own television. Bet told the viewers, 'I too, like my neighbour, come from a very large family. But now I'm the only one left. Christmas morning, usually, I spend alone, but Mrs Begum always comes round to see that I'm all right.' You might think that this was just normal good neighbourliness, except that Bet and Mrs Begum lived just around the corner from Lozells Road, a district in Birmingham where that summer there had been violent, racially motivated rioting. Shops were looted, houses set on fire.

So this was a good-news story of a kind not often shown on television, as viewers' prayers for each other passed in and out and through the small front rooms of two terraced houses in inner-city Britain. Bet and Mrs Begum, friends across what is too often thought of as a religious divide, helped many lonely people that morning, invisible behind their front doors on the day when the shops are shut, and there is no one to talk to.

Nearly 20 years later, Liz and I went back to Lozells Road, now rebuilt and teeming with people of every race and creed. It reminded us of pictures in the Bible of 1st-century Bethlehem. And here in the crowd is a new face to help people cope with loneliness and all the other pressures of inner-city life. The Reverend Jemima Prasadam, from South India, is the vicar of Lozells, a diminutive figure easily recognisable in her dog-collar and sari. She is frail, yet absolutely fearless. Jemima walks about the streets of her parish on her own, but she is never lonely, giving the peace as she calls out greetings to everyone she meets. She is happy not to have a car, preferring to pick up all the news first-hand on the street. Under her leadership, church membership is growing, but she also has the confidence and respect of Rastafarian, Hindu, Sikh and Muslim.

On Christmas Day, as she does every day, Jemima finds the lonely and bewildered strangers, legal and illegal immigrants, refugees trying to find a safe haven. Whether they stay in her parish a long time, or leave within a few days, Jemima regards them as 'her' people for as long as they are there.

O God,
from whom on different paths
all of us have come,
to whom on different paths
all of us are going,
make strong in our hearts what unites us.
Build bridges across all that divides us.
United, make us rejoice in our diversity,
at one in our witness to that peace,
which you, O God, alone can give.
ANON

As 2003 dawned, there was thankfully no curfew in Birmingham, unlike in 3rd-millennium Bethlehem, but the newsmen and their cameras were swarming all over neighbouring Aston after two teenage girls died in a shooting on the street. Once, as a young television sound-recordist, I found myself standing next to Mother Teresa of Calcutta. Overwhelmed by her extraordinary aura and the sheer immensity of the challenges she faced every day in her work for the poor, I blurted out, 'I wouldn't know where to start.'

'You start with the one standing next to you,' she replied.

chapter sixteen

Christmas at War

• • • • • • • • • • • • •

FATHER CHRISTMAS:
Here comes I, old Father Christmas.
   Christmas or not,
I hope old Father Christmas
   will never be forgot.
Make room, make room here, gallant boys,
   and give us room to rhyme;
we've come to show activity,
   upon a Christmas time.
Acting youth or acting age,
   the like was never acted on this stage;
if you don't believe what I now say,
   enter, St George, and clear the way!

ST GEORGE:
Here come I, St George the valiant man,
   with naked sword and spear in hand;
who fought the dragon and brought him to the
     slaughter,
   and for this won the king of Egypt's daughter.
What man or mortal dare to stand
   before me with my sword in hand?
I'll slay him and cut him as small as the flies,
   and send him to Jamaica to make mince-pies.

ANON, FROM A MEDIEVAL PLAY PERFORMED AT CHRISTMAS IN SUSSEX

'**M**erry Christmas, 14th Army!' The words were displayed on a streamer attached to the tail of an aircraft, and they heralded a second Christmas of fighting in Burma. As John, a retired policeman, sat on a sofa by a blazing fire to be filmed for a Christmas *Songs of Praise* from the village of Clare in Suffolk, he recalled the most unwanted seasonal greeting of his life. It meant that their enemy, the Japanese, knew exactly where they were. As John noted in the tiny diary he kept:

When they saw the Jap plane early on 25 December 1944, our fellows didn't appreciate it. We celebrated Christmas with a dinner of 'gouli' and mash, and each man had a bar of chocolate and a handful of raisins given him, and that was that.

John recalled on *Songs of Praise* what life had been like when he was making his 1944 diary entries: 'I hope no one ever has to experience another Christmas like it. Our artillery unit had just managed to cross the River Chindwin; it was a harrowing experience. Now we were hot, sweating, hungry and in a general state of unease.'

Although there has been no world war in more than 40 years of *Songs of Praise*, Christmas has never passed without news of conflict somewhere in the world. Someone somewhere has been on duty in the service of their country. Could religious broadcasting on television ever do something in the grand, old tradition of BBC radio's *Forces' Favourites* and *Two-Way Family Favourites*? This was what *Songs of Praise* director Chris Mann asked himself during the months leading up to the 1991 Gulf War, when yet another task force was being sent out to face 'heat, sweat, hunger and a general state of unease'. His answer was 'Christmas in the Gulf'.

Chris's idea was simple, direct and seemingly impossible: *Songs of Praise*, broadcast live between 11 p.m. and midnight on Christmas Eve 1990, would link up service personnel in Bahrain with their families in Germany and Aldershot. They would all hear each other via a satellite and sing carols together. Then at midnight British time – in three different time zones – they would greet one another on air. It was an engineering and security nightmare, and all the experts told him it couldn't be done. But Chris himself is a boffin who never allows mere technological complexity to get in the way of a good idea. He got his programme.

I watched the tape of that programme again on the very day in 2003 that yet another task force was setting out for the Gulf, with anxious families pictured on the television news hugging their goodbyes to loved ones. It was emotionally an almost overwhelming experience.

On *Songs of Praise* on Christmas Eve in 1990, Chris had persuaded BBC war reporter Kate Adie to gather together in the Saudi Arabian desert men from the allied troops to sing 'Silent Night'. As the reporter set off into the dark desert with her informal choir and two news cameramen, the men reminded Chris that any form of Christian worship was forbidden there.

'You'd better sing it very quietly then,' he told them.

After the carols, as midnight approached in Britain, Alan in Bahrain talked to Gloria in Aldershot as she held up their daughter, Rebecca, to the camera. 'How are you, sweetheart?' he asked his little girl, in front of the viewing millions, but Rebecca was too shy to find words for Dad. Next it was Ronnie and Sabrina's turn. Ronnie said, with laughter choking in his voice to cheer her up, 'She's crying again!' By then, so was I.

'So far away and yet so near,' said the presenter, Pam Rhodes, in Aldershot, who was acting as a television fairy godmother, making wishes come true.

In the last minute of Christmas Eve, there was a moment of pure Christmas magic, more moving than anything I have ever seen on television. Tricia in Berlin talked to her husband, on duty in the Gulf with the Seventh Armoured Brigade, the same brigade as was leaving for the Gulf again on the day I was watching the tape. She held their tiny baby daughter, Abigail, up for him to see. She was born just four days earlier and was now sleeping peacefully in Tricia's arms.

'You're gorgeous,' said the proud father to his new daughter. (Everyone was so overwhelmed by the moment that we never heard his name.) 'You're

just like your mummy. Thank you,
sweetheart. Best Christmas present any man could ever wish for.'

'Can't wait to have you back,' said Tricia.

Then the Christmas midnight candle was lit as we listened to words
from Isaiah chapter 9: 'The people that walked in darkness have seen a
great light...'

I wonder whether the presence of cameras would have changed
anything, had they been there to allow us to witness one of the strangest
moments of the First World War, on Christmas Eve 1914. In England on
that day there had been bad news: the first ever air-raid on an English town,
in which the gardener at St James's rectory in Dover, cutting green stuff to
decorate the church, was hurled 20 feet by a bomb.

Across the Channel, things were a little better: every man at the Front
received a Christmas card from the king and queen; 80 tons of Christmas
pudding had been sent over for the men in the trenches; and the pope had
called for a Christmas truce on the battlefield.

Newspapers reported that 'calm prevails on much of the Front', but the fact that in at least one sector of the front line, the enemies sang carols together and greeted each other across no-man's-land was not reported. Fraternising with the enemy, even at Christmas, would not have been tolerated.

The extraordinary story of the First World War Christmas truce is legendary. By now, however, most witnesses who survived the war are long gone. In the 1970s, researchers could still find the boys of the old brigade, and even once a Boer War survivor, for Remembrance Sunday *Songs of Praise* programmes, but although many said they'd known about it, we never met anyone who had actually taken part in that moment of

LONDON: FRIDAY, JANUARY 8, 1915.

BRITISH AND GERMANS: THE TRUCE OF CHRISTMAS.

spontaneous peace-making. However, looking through an old newspaper of the time, I have found one mention of it. On the front page of *The Daily Graphic* for Friday, 8 January 1915 are the blurred, smiling faces of men in greatcoats, standing in a snowy landscape. The image of the mixture of the spiky helmets of the Kaiser's army and the unmistakable caps of the British Expeditionary Force was a scoop for some unnamed photographer. The newspaper reported that men had written home claiming that it was the Germans who made the first move, calling out, 'Be British and meet us halfway.' It revealed that 'Tommy Atkins was soon swapping woodbines for cigars and talking desperately in Cockney, French and pidgin English.'

Within hours of this strange, spontaneous truce, the generals of both armies had ordered artillery barrages. Without the vast archive of film and television footage characteristic of modern warfare, in which we practically have a front-row seat, we can never know whether any of the unlikely Christmas Eve comrades and carol singers survived to tell the tale. But shortly afterwards, there was an appeal for British-made mouth organs to be sent out to the Front, because it was realised that many German-made models had found their way into the trenches.

Even while German cuckoo clocks were being thrown on the fire in Britain, no one could help but be moved by the story of the carol sung in one trench that Christmas night and picked up by the enemy in another trench as they recognised a familiar tune. The Germans had sung '*Stille Nacht*', a carol first sung on Christmas Eve almost a century before in the village church of St Nicholas, Oberdorf, in Austria. The allies joined in with 'Still the night, holy the night', or, as most of us now know it, 'Silent night, holy night'.

On *Songs of Praise* from the Gulf in 1990, it took the power of satellites, the BBC, the Seventh Army Brigade and Kate Adie, as well as a determined producer from *Songs of Praise*, to produce a little Christmas magic. In the unexpected calm of Christmas Eve 1914, it may be that it took only one rifleman, playing the tune on his mouth organ, to spread a message of peace and goodwill for both sides during that Christmas at war.

Stille Nacht! Heil'ge Nacht!	*Silent night, holy night!*
Alles schläft; einsam wacht	*All is calm, all is bright.*
nur das traute hoch heilige Paar.	*Round yon virgin mother and child.*
Holder Knab' im lockigten Haar,	*Holy infant so tender and mild,*
schlafe in himmlischer Ruh,	*sleep in heavenly peace,*
schlafe in himmlischer Ruh!	*sleep in heavenly peace.*
Stille Nacht! Heil'ge Nacht!	*Silent night, holy night!*
Hirten erst kundgemacht	*Shepherds quake at the sight:*
durch der Engel Alleluja,	*glories stream from heaven afar,*
Tönt es laut bei Ferne und Nah:	*heavenly hosts sing: Alleluia,*
'Jesus der Retter ist da,	*Christ the Saviour is born!*
Jesus der Retter ist da!'	*Christ the Saviour is born!*

JOSEPH MOHR (1792–1848), TRANSLATED INTO
ENGLISH BY STOPFORD A. BROOKE (1832–1916)

EPIPHANY

The Adoration of the Magi by Andrea Mantegna (1431–1506).

Look Beyond

· · · · · · · · · · · · · ·

THEN HEROD, when he had privily called the wise men, inquired of them diligently what time the star appeared. And he sent them to Bethlehem, and said, Go and search diligently for the young child; and when ye have found him, bring me word again, that I may come and worship him also. When they had heard the king, they departed; and, lo, the star, which they saw in the east, went before them, till it came and stood over where the young child was. When they saw the star, they rejoiced with exceeding great joy.

MATTHEW 2:7–10

The church I was looking for had an enticing description in John Betjeman's pocket guide to English parish churches: 'Endearing small rustic Norman; early 13th-century wall paintings.'

As I drove around the thickly wooded uplands of north-east Hampshire early one September afternoon, I found myself reliving an all-too-familiar experience from years of searching out places for future editions of *Songs of Praise*: not just the church but the whole village had vanished like Brigadoon. Even in these days of bureaucratic conformity, England's signposting remains whimsical, and without rhyme or reason, all clues to your direction will suddenly disappear at an unmarked country junction.

I had many choices of road to take, with no hint of good advice from the signwriter.

My long search for St James's in Ashmanworth that late-summer afternoon, armed with compass, map and guidebook, and with the sun still high in the western sky, came to mind later in 2003, as I was listening to a Christmas-night reflection by Archbishop Rowan Williams on the radio. He was talking about the journey of the magi to Bethlehem, and he drew on Evelyn Waugh's short story about Helena, mother of Emperor Constantine, to whom the spread of Christianity owes so much. Making her own journey to the Church of the Nativity, Helena imagines the first journeys of the shepherds and the wise men. It was the wise men who were the late arrivals, stopping to check and double-check their bearings, and taking many sightings on their complicated instruments: 'How laboriously you came, as others had run down the road; shepherds and cattle first at the stable.' But even the wise men are welcomed into the straw eventually, and they have earned a blessed accolade as patrons of all latecomers.

My search for Ashmanworth was also a sort of pilgrimage: I was searching for the spirit of a composer who had lived there. A complicated person, brimming with nervous energy, Gerald Finzi (1901–56) must also be ranked with the latecomers. Only after much distraction, delay and intermittent progress over nearly 15 years did he finally produce his wonderful work, *Dies Natalis*.

In the quiet days before Epiphany, when the overheated excitement of Christmas is done for another year, and the sound of familiar carols has become stale, Finzi's mellifluous rhapsody, a setting of inspirational words by the 17th-century priest–poet, Thomas Traherne, is my own remedy for a jaundiced spirit.

Although originally scored for soprano soloist and string orchestra, many people will know *Dies Natalis* through the recordings of the late Wilfred Brown (d. 1971). His tenor voice is instantly uplifting as soon as he begins the opening meditation on the nativity:

Will you see the infancy of this sublime and celestial greatness? I was a stranger, which at my entrance into the world was saluted and surrounded with innumerable joys; my knowledge was divine.

Finzi was born into a Jewish family. He had an unhappy childhood, and he developed into an intensely reticent man after the death of his father and all three of his brothers while he was still young. As life went on, he sought both refuge and inspiration in a romantic idea of an archetypal England, full of hidden wooded valleys and medieval churches. Finzi began to compose *Dies Natalis* in 1925, having been inspired by a Fenland church that contained rank upon rank of carved wooden angels, arching their wings over the nave.

Several years later, Finzi's son, Christopher, who was said to have been a far-from-angelic infant, was born with much celebration. He seems to have encouraged the composer back to his unfinished manuscript, and back to Traherne, who wrote, 'An empty book is like an infant's soul, in which anything may be written. It is capable of all things, but containeth nothing.'

Finzi kept on returning to his composition, which he based on Traherne's poetry and prose meditations. But even when *Dies Natalis* was finally completed in 1939, it remained largely unheard because the Second World War, which had been so feared by the composer, had begun. Like Traherne, whose work was unpublished in his own short lifetime, Finzi's rhapsodic welcome to the nativity only became widely known after his death.

Eventually, like the wise men on their journey to the stable in Bethlehem, I came upon Ashmanworth. A village green appeared, but there was still no sign of the 'endearing small rustic Norman church' that stood next to the house where *Dies Natalis* was finally finished. As for many an ancient holy place, St James's Church is not in the village but up a secluded track. I wondered how on earth the audience had found its way there on 28 December 1940, Holy Innocents' Day, when Finzi had launched a newly formed orchestra there.

It was as unpromising a start for an orchestra as the birth in the stable, what with wartime blackout conditions and conducting by Finzi, who admitted, 'I shall never make much of a conductor.' Yet the amateurs of the Newbury String Players broke new ground with their hour of music in the candlelit church that December. For almost the next 40 years, the Ashmanworth concert was a fixed part of the Christmas tradition, and it helped encourage thousands of other churches, which now regularly open their doors to music-lovers.

I longed to go and look inside, but as the summer sun began to set, I was alone, circling the old church with its outcrops of mellow brick. By the south door, I found a plain but elegant memorial to the man whose music has inspired pilgrimages to St James's from all over the world. The door was locked, however, and there was nobody to let me in. Overhead, the graveyard's rooks and crows were having difficulty competing with the throbbing sounds of pop music emanating from a nearby farm.

On the point of admitting my pilgrimage had failed and starting the car, I became aware of a huge flower arrangement speeding through the churchyard, and I went in hot pursuit. I am grateful to the young flower arranger for not locking the pursuing stranger out.

The church's interior was light and welcoming, with a good acoustic for a string orchestra, yet it was also cool and astonishingly tiny. The cleverest *Songs of Praise* outside-broadcast camera planner would have been defeated by it. There must have been a terrible crush on that candlelit afternoon of the first concert. But perhaps for Finzi, always nervous of a threatening, wider world, its very smallness, rusticity and 'endearing' atmosphere made it an ideal, safe space for his music to be performed.

Finzi and his musicians were not altogether welcomed by the host church in 1940, and there were some complaints, all too familiar to a *Songs o Praise* producer, by some of those present. The composer noted afterwards:

Mrs S. of our village was horrified that Mrs W., a confirmed unbeliever, should come into the church to hear the music, and went as far as to say she should not have been allowed in. Mrs W., on the other hand, was appalled at the vicar's prayers, which she thought quite out of place.

Finzi also wrote:

I didn't rejoice that only four people go to church on a Sunday, and 100 came to hear music on a weekday... I did rejoice to think that, perhaps for the first time in its history, most of the chapel attended the church, and that agnostics, RCs, Anglo-Cs, Jews and C of Es were all gathered together with all their ridiculous differences dropped for at least one hour.

That could have been a manifesto for *Songs of Praise*, a series that was to begin life in 1962, and which is now hopeful of reaching its half-century.

As I left, I noticed a bench for visitors. On its back were carved the words 'Look beyond'. They seemed appropriate for the church that sheltered

the composer of *Dies Natalis*, a work that looks at and beyond Christmas. These are the words around which he first began his composition in 1925:

These little limbs, these eyes and hands which here I find,
  this panting heart wherewith my life begins;
where have ye been? Behind what curtain were ye from me hid so long?
  where was, in what abyss, my new-made tongue?

When silent I so many thousand thousand years
  beneath the dust did in a chaos lie, how could I smiles, or tears,
or lips or hands, or eyes, or ears perceive?
  Welcome, ye treasures which I now
    receive.

From dust I rise and out of nothing now
    awake,
  these brighter regions which salute my eyes,
a gift from God I take, the earth, the seas,
    the light, the lofty skies,
  the sun and stars are mine; if these I prize.

A stranger here strange things doth meet,
    strange glory see,
  strange treasures lodged in this fair world appear,
strange, all, and new to me: but that they mine should be who nothing was,
  that strangest is of all; yet brought to pass.

'THE SALUTATION' BY THOMAS TRAHERNE (1637–74), FROM *DIES NATALIS* BY GERALD FINZI (1901–56)

chapter eighteen

Hogmanay
Past and Present

● ● ● ● ● ● ● ● ● ● ● ● ●

IT IS SHREWDLY SUSPECTED that the number of fresh applicants to Prosopographus [a silhouette artist] arises from their desire to present their likeness to friends and relatives as New Year gifts. And can there be a more pleasing or rational offering than striking resemblances of those we love and esteem?

GIFT SUGGESTION FROM *THE SCOTSMAN*, NEW YEAR 1821

Sir Walter Scott appears to be in a pensive mood. A few yards away, Provost Alexander Black is looking thunderous. It is New Year's Eve, Hogmanay to the Scots, and brightly lit fairground booths have come to Princes Street and engulfed both of these old Edinburgh worthies, who are now enshrined in stone. Sir Walter, sheltered by the slender spire of his elegant monument, stands next to a giant ferris wheel that dances with lights, a giant cobweb revolving revellers high over the city. Far below, in the Princes Street Gardens, ice skaters in colourful, flying scarves waltz round and round to booming music over ground normally occupied by demure corporation grass.

The world comes to Scotland to celebrate Auld Lang Syne. New Year's Eve has always granted the dour Presbyterian nation a rare chance to let its hair down, and they do it with magnificent abandon. Breathless television news reporters tell us each year that greater crowds than ever are cramming into the city. The lager goes down and 10 tons of fireworks go up. As the credit-card debts mount for the city's visitors, Sir Walter, looking down from his monument, may well be remembering his own regularly impecunious state during this season.

Today, the city is booming and prosperous. This winter festival of lights begins before Christmas and continues through to the New Year. Provost Black's successor, the present Lord Provost of Edinburgh, shares none of his predecessor's Presbyterian disapproval of fun, and on New Year's Eve, he is out in the streets with the crowds at midnight, exchanging greetings with tourists from far and wide.

Like many children, I grew up with stories of a beautiful, lost world. The 'old days' were gone, and somehow it was all the fault of the young. We were the 'new, selfish' generation, who almost as soon as we had taken our first breath were somehow spoiling creation. The story of Adam and Eve sunk in at a very early age.

'You will never know what you've missed,' my grandmother would say triumphantly. Having a contrary nature, I took this as a challenge to find out for myself. Did we really have nothing to compare with what our ancestors knew? I began to consume history books, and there are still few greater pleasures for the now 'old, selfish' me than to lose myself in a collection of yellowing newspapers.

Until 50 years ago, Christmas Day was a working day for most Scots. It was barely even celebrated as a Christian festival, because of Presbyterian disapproval of anything that smacked of idolatry. In December 1822, Sir Walter had high hopes for the sales of what *The Scotsman* newspaper called his 'Christmas gift': the annual publication of a new story in the tradition of his Waverly novels.

In the leading article of the New Year's Eve edition of *The Scotsman* that year, the writer observed:

In a season when the evening is perhaps too much wasted in social indulgence, it is somewhat hard to employ the morning in imagination. There is more hardship still in being compelled – as newspaper critics are – to give opinions before we have had time to reflect on what has been read. Yet we must not quarrel with such a Christmas gift…

An evening 'wasted in social indulgence' doesn't sound like too much fun. And how extraordinary it would be today if we had to wait until after Christmas before opinions were aired in the media about a newly published Harry Potter title from J.K. Rowling, Edinburgh's current successor to Sir Walter as a purveyor of magic.

'Our New Year revels have been both general and deep – the mirth a little boisterous, but no lack of good humour,' reported *The Scotsman* pompously in 1823. It was less generous with Sir Walter's latest offering, *St Ronan's Well*:

At the outset, the word of the magician was visible, but the dialogue soon became more studied… the sauce piquante abandoned more than it was wont and the composition became altogether more sarcastic.

In *St Ronan's Well*, Sir Walter gives us a glimpse of a Presbyterian New Year at the beginning of the 19th century. It was a far less cheerful affair than today's celebrations. *The Scotsman*'s critic found fault with the novel's absent-minded and contrary Reverend Mr Cargill, who flits in and out of the plot, and is 'of vulgar material and ludicrous habit'. We can certainly hope that no modern-day divine would so misjudge matters as the Reverend Mr Cargill, who when 'preaching a last sermon before a party of criminals condemned to death, [broke] off by promising the wretches who were to suffer next morning, "the rest of the discourse at the first proper opportunity"'. Nevertheless, the critic concluded, no doubt to the author's great relief, 'this is a story that you will not put down at bedtime until it be finished'.

New Year's Eve in Princes Street, Edinburgh, with the monument to Sir Walter Scott behind the ferris wheel.

Just before the Tran Kirk Clock chimes the last midnight of the old year, and 'Tom the Gun' heralds the start of the new one, through the miracle of modern technology, Big Ben in London is emerging ghost-like through the smoke of the Edinburgh fireworks onto our television screens to bong us into the new year. Out in the city, all the old clocks chime, fireworks whizz off into the air, and the crowds embrace strangers and laugh and sing. It is time to raise our glasses to our dear, departed grandparents and say, 'This is still a beautiful world.'

Time, like an ever-rolling stream,
  bears all its sons away;
they fly forgotten, as a dream
  dies at the opening day.

O God, our help in ages past,
  our hope for years to come,
be thou our guard while troubles last,
  and our eternal home.

FROM 'O GOD, OUR HELP IN AGES PAST' BY
ISAAC WATTS (1674–1748), BASED ON PSALM 90

The Big Ben Minute

chapter nineteen

RING OUT, wild bells, to the wild sky…

Ring out the old, ring in the new,
   ring, happy bells, across the snow:
   the year is going, let him go;
ring out the false, ring in the true.

'CVI' FROM *IN MEMORIAM A.H.H.* BY
ALFRED LORD TENNYSON (1809–92)

One invariable feature of my own childhood experience of New Year at home in South London was that we would always miss Big Ben. As midnight approached, all the local Scots exiles, crammed into our living room and corralled by our half-Scots family, were in high spirits. It was not until the last minute that anyone would remember we were in a house full of clocks that, ticking the old year away merrily, all showed different times. Somebody would dial 'Tim', the speaking clock, but in spite of lots of sh-sh-shing, the party hubbub was always far too great to hear the familiar 'precisely' or the 'third stroke' of the pips. Somebody else with a clearer head would then rush and turn on the radio.

If I was lucky, I caught the last bong of Big Ben on the BBC Home Service. I always felt that in missing Big Ben, we were missing an important rite of passage, a vital moment of history. As I plaintively announced the new year's arrival over the merry accordions of our one-and-only Jimmy Shand LP, my mother would call in surprise, 'Oh, did we miss it?' and then everyone would add to the uncharacteristic din in our South London suburb with as much of 'Auld Lang Syne' as we could remember.

Big Ben's booming chimes have been broadcast all round the world to mark significant moments in our lives. On Remembrance Sunday 1940, the chimes broadcast just before the nine o'clock evening news had a new meaning for many listeners gathered behind their black-out curtains. The launch of the Big Ben silent minute followed the worst months of the wartime blitz, and as the BBC announcer said just before the hour:

There is no doubt that we must face the future courageously, that we must build for the future wherever we may; above all that we must find fresh standards on which to build, and some will be seeking those standards as Big Ben strikes.

It was the oddest religious broadcast ever dreamed up, a minute of radio silence except for the booming of the great clock, and it was a victory for a listener who had persuaded the BBC not to speak over or fade out the chimes, a custom which lasted for the next 20 years or more.

It all began in December 1917, when two comrades at the Front in Palestine talked through the night before a battle. One said:

I shall not come through this war. You will survive and live to see a greater and more final conflict. When that time comes, remember us who have gone on ahead. We shall be an unseen and mighty army. Give us the chance to pull our weight. You will still have time available as your servant – lend us a moment of it each day, and through your silence give us your opportunity. The power of silence is greater than you know. When those tragic days arrive, do not forget us.

The next day, the speaker died in battle, but his companion, Major W. Tudor Pole, said that he never forgot his friend's words.

When the letter from Major Pole arrived in 1940, the BBC found all sorts of ways of worrying about his proposal, which was that one minute of prayer should lead up to the chimes each night. The governors veered between unease at hosting a national religious revival and fears that it could be used by enemy spies to send coded messages. What would be the effect on morale, they wondered, if bombs could be heard during the chimes? But the unstoppable Major Pole eventually persuaded the BBC to allow the silent minute to take place so that everyone could have their own thoughts while Big Ben struck.

People discovered that the Lord's Prayer said slowly fitted into the chimes, but the BBC would not agree to broadcasting it, and after all, Major Pole's comrade had spoken of the power of silence.

Even today, in my own hectic, disorganised schedule, I often stop for a moment's reflection when I hear a clock chiming or church bells ringing. On New Year's Eve, before the welcoming hugs, I have my own silent minute.

I said to the man who stood at
the Gate of the Year,
'Give me a light that I may tread
safely into the unknown.'
And he replied, 'Go out into the
darkness, and put your hand
into the hand of God.
That shall be to you better than
light,
and safer than a known way.'

'THE GATE OF THE YEAR' FROM 'GOD KNOWS' BY MINNIE LOUISE HASKINS (1875–1957); READ BY KING GEORGE VI IN HIS CHRISTMAS BROADCAST OF 1939

chapter twenty

Porridge and Old Clothes

· · · · · · · · · · · · ·

WELL, SO THAT IS THAT. Now we must dismantle the tree,
putting the decorations back into their cardboard boxes –
some have got broken – and carrying them up into the attic.
The holly and the mistletoe must be taken down and burnt,
and the children got ready for school. There are enough
left-overs to do, warmed up, for the rest of the week –
not that we have much appetite, having drunk such a lot,
stayed up so late, attempted – quite unsuccessfully –
to love all our relatives, and in general
grossly overestimated our powers…

FROM 'THE FLIGHT INTO EGYPT', FROM *FOR THE TIME BEING* (1944) BY W.H. AUDEN (1909–73)

On twelfth night, my father always used to say, 'Time to go back to porridge and old clothes.' I used to wait in dread for him to say it. It was not so much his words as the grim note of resignation in his voice, which seemed to herald an endless time of dull duty and routine ahead, all unexpected adventures packed away for another year. In actual fact, porridge was rather a treat in our home, and it would usually mark a day of exceptional excitement, such as when we had all woken up to find an overnight snowfall had magically transformed our suburban garden into a winter wonderland. Even then, my father was back in his old 'demob' overcoat, mournfully rooting about in the coal shed for any respectable-sized lumps in the slack and dross – which was all that post-war coal merchants seemed to deliver. 'Can one of you boys give him a hand?'

my mother would call. The Christmas tree, so magical when we set it up, was now looking sad and protesting at its treatment by shedding furiously all over the carpet as it was evicted. It would lie in the snow, a sad and reproachful icon of missed opportunities, one or two tired decorations still entangled in its branches, waving a final goodbye to our fun.

... Once again
as in previous years we have seen the actual Vision and failed
to do more than entertain it as an agreeable
possibility, once again we have sent him away,
begging though to remain his disobedient servant,
the promising child who cannot keep his word for long.
FROM 'THE FLIGHT INTO EGYPT', FROM *FOR THE TIME BEING* (1944) BY W.H. AUDEN (1909–73)

As a child, I would make my annual New Year's resolution to say goodbye to whining Mr Nasty and hello to the helpful Mr Good-as-Gold. But soon after the arrival of the wise men at our sitting-room nativity scene and their speedy departure back into the cupboard under the stairs on twelfth night, it was already clear that I had better not give up the day job.

And yet 'porridge and old clothes', forgetting my father's doom-filled tones for a moment, could be a good description of the man in the first chapter of Mark's Gospel, who dressed in camel hair and ate locusts and wild honey. That uncomfortable prophet, John the Baptist, with his wild appearance, comes just at the right time to help with New Year resolve. He bursts into our post-Christmas blues; his story is read in churches just a week after the wise men have come and gone. W.H. Auden holds up a mirror in which we have all failed, but John the Baptist comes to show us how to start again. In the inner wildernesses we create for ourselves, John comes with the news that if we repent, we will be forgiven, and after that everything will change. God forgives us, even when we cannot forgive ourselves.

Just before Advent 2002, I was in Bosnia. There can be few places in

Bishop Franjo Komarica with the statue of Joseph.

the world where God's forgiveness is more needed. Here Catholic and Orthodox Christians once lived in harmony. Christians and Muslims were neighbours. Now, after the country has torn itself apart, with churches and mosques blown up, priests murdered and thousands dead or displaced from their homes, the people of Bosnia are having to start again. People are still traumatised by what was done to them and their families, but they are almost more traumatised by what they know they themselves did to others during five years of fear and violence.

There, I met Bishop Franjo Komarica, who had been kept under house arrest for a year when the former Yugoslavia had disintegrated into a state of civil war. The bishop spoke no English, but I learned something about forgiveness from what he showed us in his diocese of Banja Luka, where people of all faiths are still struggling to 'get back to normal', and to their own equivalent of 'porridge and old clothes'.

In his home, the bishop held out a beautiful statue of Joseph for us to see. This dreamer of angels had stood by his wife, Mary, in another perilous time, and he had been exquisitely carved from a single piece of wood. The unknown artist had created a face that expressed tranquillity. Then the bishop parted his hands, and we saw that the statue had been shattered into two pieces – shocking evidence of a violent time. But as quickly as he pulled the two pieces apart, he gently pressed them together again. That gesture was all we needed to see how this passionate Catholic bishop intended to heal some of the deep wounds of the people of Bosnia.

The statue had survived the bullet and bayonet blow that split it in two, and as I watched Bishop Franjo looking at Joseph's scarred but tranquil face, there seemed to be a silent understanding between them.

Fifty years on from my childhood gloom, I still love Christmas, but I am now also glad when the feast is past, and we can all get back to work. Graham Forbes, the provost of St Mary's Cathedral, Edinburgh, who preached on St John the Baptist Sunday 2003 that 'John, the voice, points away from himself to Christ, the Word', neither spoke nor appeared himself in the *Watch*

Night Service, broadcast from the cathedral by BBC Scotland. He preferred to trust 500 children from the city to tell viewers the story, with carols and readings, of God's coming to earth. Like John the Baptist, the provost preferred to point away from himself, not up to the sky, but to someone on earth, or in this case to 500 children, in whose faces viewers might see the face of the child in the manger.

Small wonder the star, small wonder the light,
the angels in chorus, the shepherds in fright;
but stable and manger for God – no small wonder!

Small wonder the kings, small wonder they bore
the gold and the incense, the myrrh, to adore;
but God gives his life on a cross – no small wonder!

Small wonder the love, small wonder the grace,
the power, the glory, the light of his face;
but all to redeem my poor heart – no small wonder!

'NO SMALL WONDER' BY PAUL WIGMORE (1925–)